# ORGANIZING FRIENDS GROUPS

## A How-To-Do-It Manual for Librarians

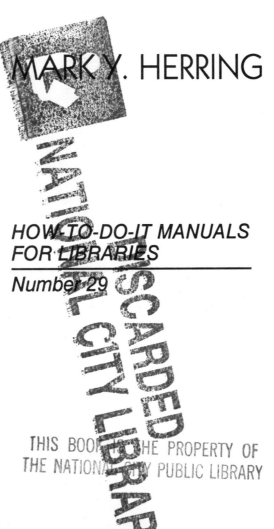

## MARK Y. HERRING

### HOW-TO-DO-IT MANUALS FOR LIBRARIES
*Number 29*

**NEAL-SCHUMAN PUBLISHERS, INC.**
New York, London

Published by Neal-Schuman Publishers, Inc.
100 Varick Street
New York, NY 10013

Printed and bound in the United States of America

**Library of Congress Cataloging-in-Publication Data**

Herring, Mark Youngblood.
    Organizing friends groups : a how-to-do-it manual for librarians /
Mark Y. Herring.
        p. cm. — (How-to-do-it manuals for libraries ; no. 29)
    Includes bibliographical references and index.
    ISBN 1-55570-062-4
    1. Friends of the library—United States.    I. Title.    II. Series.
Z681.5.H47   1992
021.7—dc20                                                                92-40785
                                                                              CIP

*Amici usque ad aras*
(Friends to the last)

# CONTENTS

# FOREWORD

Before reading this book, I might have said, "We don't need another work on library Friends groups." But this book is so well-conceived and presents such a compelling case for increasing the number of Friends groups that I am convinced of the real need for this work. No current book provides the same information in such a clear, precise format as you will find in *Organizing Friends Groups.*

The book is specific in focus, offering depth and insight. The early chapters discuss leadership and management styles, vital matters of concern to organizers of Friends groups. These sections are one of the great strengths of this book. The author has researched the Friends thoroughly and has presented the subject in exacting detail, from the writing of the constitution and by-laws to the planning, budgeting, and staging of the annual event. An added feature is the set of practical exercises offered at the end of each chapter.

Directors (and aspiring directors) of smaller libraries will find *Organizing Friends Groups* a valuable blueprint for starting a Friends group. It is also a useful guide for existing Friends groups that need changing or revitalizing.

Charlene K. Clark
Development and Promotion Coordinator
Texas A&M University

# PREFACE

More than a decade ago, as I sat in a class on academic librarianship, I dutifully made notes on that day's lecture: "Friends Groups of Academic Libraries." While making the customary notes, I editorialized, as was my habit, in the margins. After a few remarks by the professor on the types of programs being hosted by some Friends groups, I wrote the following: "Insipid idea. Never do this." The words, so far as I know, are still in my notes. I should have known then that one never says never.

About three years later, I sat in the catbird seat as the newly appointed director of a small, private liberal arts college library in an even smaller rural town in northeast Tennessee. Although the college had been in this town for nearly 120 years, I ran into people who claimed not to know there was a library on our campus that the community could use. I had been out of brilliant ideas for increasing the library's budget and our exposure in the community when an "insipid" idea struck me. If we could implement a Friends group, perhaps that would show the administration that we were trying as hard as we could to increase the library's financial stability. It would also wake up the larger community to the fact that we were there. That insipid idea was a success beyond my wildest expectations.

In a town nestled in the Appalachian mountain range, the Friends group I helped start made about $60,000 in less than six years. Focusing on an annual speaker-dinner event, we brought in the likes of Alex Haley, John Ehrlichman, Kathryn Koob (one of the two female hostages held in Iran), Michael Novak, William F. Buckley, Jr., and Arthur Schlesinger, Jr. We began the program without a budget, and ran it on the year's previous "take." I think I can safely say that we were a huge success and put our academic library on the map. We made mistakes (many of which were owing to my unsure hand), but we did what we set out to do: establish the library as a cultural force, not only on the campus to which it was attached, but also to the community in which the college resided.

What plagued me in the early going, however, was how to start this group. Nearly everything I read (and I did read just about everything then written on the subject) remained somewhat remote. A spate of materials existed on tax-exempt status, incorporating the group, types of programs, and publicity. It seemed to me that I was on an island trying to get off and the only books being sent me in response to my bottled messages were *Robinson Crusoe* and *Treasure Island*, rather than the requisite *Shipbuilding Made Easy*.

This brings me to the first reason I wrote this book: to provide would-be Friends organizers with some nuts and bolts materials about how to begin from the proverbial square one. While my experience is no doubt personal, it does not follow that it is altogether unusual. I have tried to show that with Friends groups, as Dr. Johnson once wrote with respect to another matter, what is known is not always obvious, and what is obvious is not always known. How often I wished in those early days for a book like this one. It would have given me, at the very least, something of a map that I could follow.

The primary focus of *Organizing Friends Groups: A How-To-Do-It Manual for Librarians* is an annual speaker-dinner event. This does not mean that I think this is the only event a Friends group could or should host. It is merely the one with which I have had the most experience. One could write numerous books on scores of different Friends programs. Although this book's focus is a narrow one, the ideas offered to make this type of annual event work may be adapted for just about any other event a Friends group might choose to undertake.

I have tried, in the organization of this book, not only to describe the process, but to point out numerous pitfalls that may occur. I have also tried to learn from my mistakes and describe, rather than just the failures, what I might have done to prevent them. For example, one of the most difficult tasks in the whole Friends process is putting together the organizing committee and selecting a Friends leader. It is no easy task finding members for that committee who will have as much energy and enthusiasm as you will have; in fact you shouldn't expect to do so. But members can be found who will work hard for the goals and objectives prescribed for them.

Finding the Friends leader is another story, harder still than finding members for the organizing committee. I would have appreciated a book that told me there would be days like this in the structure of a Friends group. Friends of the Library, USA, is a marvelous organization and will bend over backwards to help. But it cannot do everything. Sometimes a book that simply lets you know that you are not alone works wonders.

This book also focuses on participatory management and its importance in the organization and continuation of a Friends group. Participatory management is a difficult task to implement, but who can doubt its usefulness, not only here but in the larger organization and administration of the library? If the collapse of Eastern Europe has taught us anything it has been this: failure to allow for ego involvement in any enterprise will lead to its ultimate failure.

This book also tries to be realistic. The admonition here is always the same: get started on that Friends group. Unlike most of the books that I encountered, which left me blissfully ignorant of the difficulty of the Friends enterprise, this one admits freely that certain tasks may not be as easy as falling off logs.

The book is organized from the point of view of the Friends-wannabe who thinks that a Friends organization would be a good idea to discuss with others. Each chapter records, chronologically, the steps to follow in the process. At the end of each chapter is a "Things to Do" section to help readers make the transition from learning to doing. These tasks can be done as exercises or "for real," as part and parcel of the process of Friends building. The bibliography is intended to provide a starting place for people who want to read further.

This book is appropriate for use in connection with an academic, public, or special library. Since my experience has been with academic libraries, most of my examples are in that setting, but I also provide some examples set in other types of libraries.

Some Friends books provide brief information on putting together a group. Still others encourage, prod, and laud those who attempt the undertaking. Few books, however, provide readers with the kind of detailed information this book provides. While I cannot guarantee that using this book will ensure a successful Friends venture every time, I believe I can promise that if you follow its prescriptions with some care, your chances of success will be greatly enhanced.

This book, like many others, requires some acknowledgments. First, from the bottom of my heart, I thank my editor, Pat Read. With a name like Read, how could an author go wrong? Of course all of the blunders are mine, but Pat's eagle eye tagged those unreadable portions for prompt revision.

I would be greatly remiss if I did not thank my family for their encouragement and support during the writing of this book. Many thanks are also offered to Neal-Schuman Publishers, especially its president, Pat Schuman. The contract for this book came during the middle of three very difficult years for me. Such times do not make for the best copy, nor the most exacting promptitude, but Neal-Schuman has been very understanding.

Finally, many thanks must go to five very important women, without whose help the Friends group we began would never have survived. In alphabetical order they are Betty Curtis, Ann Peake, Lila Ray, Anna Slagle, and Sharon Volkman. While they may not recognize everything here, they are sure to recognize the spirit of their efforts throughout this book.

# PREPARING FOR A FRIENDS GROUP

Friends of libraries exist for a variety of reasons. No one best form or type of Friends group exists. The type of Friends group that is best-suited to your library will largely depend on what you, along with a cast of nearly thousands, decide it ought to be. You determine this by finding, first of all, a person who is energetic about the library and about the Friends group—a person with a vision and a mission for such a group. You match that person up with a number of others who serve on a steering committee, made up of individuals representing a number of varied concerns: students, faculty, administrators, and community members. (The primary focus of this book is *academic* libraries, but Friends groups in public libraries will also be covered where possible. In the case of public libraries, the strategy for starting a steering committee is the same, but with differing groups: trustees, patrons, and the community at large.)

Once the steering committee has done its work and turned the reins over to a Friends executive board (made up of some of the members from the steering committee and some new ones), you continue to bring into that Friends group people who are equally enthusiastic about the library and who want to see the group succeed. Along the way, members receive numerous benefits by meeting with individuals with mutual interests. The library receives many benefits, too, some in the form of money, others in the form of publicity, advocacy, services, or programs. The entire enterprise is limited only by your members' imaginations.

Sound simple? Well, it is and it isn't. Before I get too far ahead of myself, some background information may be in order. According to the most recent statistics available, there are just over 3,500 academic institutions in the United States. Every one of these institutions *could* have a Friends of the Library organization, but the sad truth is that most do not. In fact, according to the most recent figures from Friends of Libraries USA (FOLUSA), only about 2,000 libraries of *any* description have Friends groups. Many of these are *public* libraries. In order to get a more accurate estimate of the number of Friends groups associated with academic libraries, we need to look further still.

A 1987 study by Ronnelle Thompson[1] is anything but optimistic on this point. Thompson found that of 136 college libraries surveyed, only 33, or 24 percent, had Friends groups associated with them. Friends of academic libraries exist, but they could hardly be called a universal institution in academia. Nor are many Friends groups large organizations. Only about 400 of *all* Friends groups have more than 350 members. Most academic Friends groups, then, are small organizations designed around some rallying point. Perhaps one reason these groups are slow to form may be a common hesitancy and lack of knowledge about how to form them. This book is designed to help overcome that hesitancy by offering suggestions on how to begin a Friends group in an academic library. Examples from public library Friends groups should provide readers with some information for beginning groups in that setting as well.

The Friends groups that are currently in existence are nothing short of robust. The foci of these groups are as varied as one could imagine. It would appear that what a Friends group does within a college is limited only by what those in the group decide *not* to do. Not only are the activities of all these Friends groups widely varied, but so is what they do with their funding.

At Southern Illinois University in Edwardsville, for example, the Friends of the Library group focuses on one annual benefit for the library that often brings in thousands of dollars. Throughout the year the library also holds other special events that might focus on one of the library's collections or a guest speaker. Funds raised from these events have paid for the renovation of the library's rare book reading room and the development of collections in world literature, women's studies, and African-American studies.

At the Emmanuel School of Religion, located in northeast Tennessee, one finds a very loosely organized "Friends" group. (The word "Friends" is in quotation marks for a reason.) Friends contributing to the library are bound by no constitution, no by-laws, and rarely meet. Yet thanks to the efforts of one professor, one women's group, and the librarian, the library has been the recipient of more than $200,000 over the last 25 years. The New Testament Seminar Collection now boasts thousands of scholarly titles in its area and is housed in a separate section of the library. The "Fig Tree," a women's group, while focusing its work on the entire campus, has contributed about $9,000 each year to the library since 1975. "Volumeteers," an outreach of the Fig Tree group, are retired men and women who come to the library to help catalog books, affix labels, and shelve new titles. When one considers that ESR has no more than 150 students in any given semester, the effort seems all the more grand.

Of course, Friends of the Library organizations have long been a mainstay at public libraries. The Friends of the Johnson City, Tennessee, Public Library is run by an entirely separate board of directors, with the library director serving as an ex officio member of the board. This group sponsors "Third Thursday" programs featuring local guest speakers. While "Third Thursday" functions as a public relations effort, this Friends group also raises funds for the library through the contributions of nearly 200 members, annual book sales of discarded or unused gift books, and an annual Author-Dinner event. The library also sponsors an "Outstanding Achievement Award in the Arts and Humanities." The sale of book bags, tee shirts, stationery, and other memorabilia is another fundraising effort.

The Friends of the Tompkins County (N.Y.) Public Library began nearly 50 years ago. Their first event, a book sale, netted less than $500. The 1990 book sale grossed nearly $80,000. This annual event attracts interested book buyers from all over the county. From very modest beginnings, the library has benefitted over the years to the tune of around $400,000!

Of more recent vintage is the Vashon, Washington, Friends of the Library group, which began in the early eighties with about 150 members. Vashon has a distinctive feature that, while adding to its allure, does not exactly increase its Friends potential. No, it isn't that the population is barely 8,000, though that is true. It's that Vashon requires a ferry ride to get to the island! But has inaccessibility prevented a Friends program from developing? Hardly! Book sales are again the Vashon Friends' main activity. Held in conjunction with a summer festival, the book sale makes about $1,000 each year. Add to this the revenue generated from Friends membership (several hundred dollars) and it makes for a very successful Friends venture. Vashon Friends have used their money to purchase an IBM typewriter for use (at 50 cents an hour) by the public.

Small colleges are also in on the Friends act. The Gustavus Library Associates of Gustavus Adolphus College won the 1990 FOLUSA Award for its extraordinary achievements in fundraising via their "A Royal Affair—Holiday Magic" event. This event featured a silent auction, dinner, and entertainment. The college received more than $100,000 for its well-organized efforts.

Even at particularly small college libraries, Friends activities are ongoing, energetic, and exciting. At King College, a liberal arts college of only 500 students and less than 120,000 volumes in northeast Tennessee, the Friends of the Library of King College raised more than $50,000 via six annual dinner-speaker events. The King Library hosted speaking giants such as Alex Haley, John Ehrlichman, Kathryn Koob (the former Iranian hostage), Michael Novak, William F. Buckley, Jr., and Arthur Schlesinger, Jr.—all in a community of less than 40,000.

As you can see, whether at a large university, a small special library, a medium-sized public library, or a very small college library, Friends groups are alive and vibrant. It is also easy to see that whatever the library, Friends groups exist for a variety of reasons: fundraising, social gatherings, public relations, advocacy, and many others. If you decide you want to get together with some friends and explore the Friends process, you could be considered innovative and ground-breaking, considering the small numbers above. Suppose you are thinking, "Well, why not? Where do I go from here?" Let us examine what is needed first to get the Friends ball rolling.

## MISSION AND PURPOSE

The first two things you need to begin a Friends group are a leader with a vision and a mission for the Friends group. A vision is like a prophet's dream. It is an unrestricted, even wild, hope that certain things will come to pass. Unlike the prophet, you probably won't have a divine inspiration that certain things will occur. But you must have the fire of desire to see that those things you want to occur will have every opportunity to do so. You must also be able to convince others that they should want them to occur too.

The mission is the road map to the vision. For the sake of libraries and Friends groups, it may be said to be the *purpose* of the Friends group (fundraising, advocacy, public relations, etc.). It is all very well and good to have a vision, but if there aren't ways of getting from point A to point B, success will be imaginary. After all, Jacob did at least have a ladder! The mission must provide this "ladder" in order to get to the vision, and the ladder must prove to be accessible to all the members involved. It is the leader's responsibility to furnish both vision and mission, both ladder and accessibility.

The leader of a library Friends group could be the director of the library, an administrator, a library staff member, or a person either inside or outside the library community. This person has to be willing to "jump-start" the group by offering the "rallying point." The rallying point will help bring together representative members from the library community to plan and decide on the specific focus of your Friends group. In academic libraries, this means students, faculty, staff, administrators, and alumni. For public libraries, it means representatives from the board of trustees, the community, and the media (more about this committee in chapter 2).

Friends groups do not exist *exclusively* for the purpose of raising much-needed extra funding for libraries, although they obviously serve that purpose quite nicely. They really are more of a doing-what-has-to-be-done mechanism. Friends groups do allow librarians to ask for funds while at the same time taking the sting out of the asking. (In fact, Friends groups make the process rather fun.) But if fundraising is not what your group wants or needs (or is allowed to do), then there are other activities that might serve as a valuable focus for your organization.

# FOCUSING YOUR GROUP

Friends groups are formed for five basic *purposes*: volunteer services, library awareness or literacy, public relations, advocacy, and fundraising.[2]

## VOLUNTEER SERVICES FRIENDS GROUPS

Friends groups may provide volunteer services for the library, for the community, or both. Of course, volunteers cannot replace professional staff in the library any more than they can in any other enterprise. But volunteers can provide invaluable services. Friends groups designed to provide a pool of volunteers for the library may meet infrequently, require little library director or library staff responsibility, and may or may not have by-laws, committees, or elected officers. Of course, such groups often do have these things, but others may not go to the extra effort of constituting themselves in a formal manner. They are able to follow an informal set of rules that govern their meetings, when they decide to meet. It should be noted, however, that Friends groups that do not go to the extra trouble of writing a constitution and by-laws may be positioning themselves for an early death. It isn't that the constitution and by-laws give the group life, but the *process* of putting them together gives the group the early sense of legitimacy that can be beneficial.

These volunteer groups perform tasks such as placing bar codes on books for the library's new circulation system or helping with the library's year-end inventory. Assigned to staff members, they may come in once a week or once a month and help with day-to-day activities or long-term projects. Whatever they do, volunteers provide much needed services.

## LIBRARY AWARENESS OR LITERACY FRIENDS GROUPS

Friends groups that focus on library awareness bring to the community, both academic and public, the *sine qua non* of libraries: reading. While almost everyone speaks favorably of libraries, not everyone knows why they are needed or why their functions need to be preserved.

Educational and cultural enrichment is another important reason why Friends groups are formed. Groups may meet to view the films of a member's recent trip to another country, or to look at a member's collection of anything from seashells to stamps. This kind of group might even host a program about the national illiteracy problem or specific concerns about illiteracy in their community. These groups may not meet frequently, are usually small, and often require little library staff involvement. But because the library provides a convenient meeting place for the group, library staff will have to be involved to some degree.

## PUBLIC RELATIONS FRIENDS GROUPS

Friends groups organized for public relations do for libraries what Madison Avenue does for commercial enterprises. These groups may be large and often have elected officers, but not in every case. Their chief task is making sure the local and/or campus community knows the library is there to serve them. Such groups often play up the library's collections and contributions to the community, thus indirectly attracting local businesses to contribute to the library's ongoing services. For example, a group might highlight their library's online search services, encouraging businesses to help fund them. In this way, these groups can fill a library's fundraising as well as public relations needs.

## ADVOCACY FRIENDS GROUPS

Advocacy Friends groups mobilize citizens to lobby for the preservation of libraries and library services. These groups are usually associated with public libraries, but not always. Such groups may meet to publicize the need for libraries, why libraries need to be preserved, or what local residents can do politically to assist in their library's growth. Advocacy Friends groups may become very involved politically, supporting tax measures and attempting to thwart counter-tax initiatives (such as California's Proposition 13). Library staffs, for that reason, will want to examine whether or not they can afford (or can afford not) to be involved with groups that may polarize citizens on a given issue.

The current anti-tax sentiment makes libraries in upcoming political races especially vulnerable.

## FUNDRAISING FRIENDS GROUPS

Although mentioned last, fundraising groups are the main focus of this book. Fundraising groups may be large or small, and they usually have a written constitution and by-laws and elected officers. Elected officers include a president, a vice-president, a secretary, a treasurer, and a program director. Fundraising groups may lengthen or shorten this list as needed.

Such groups usually also have committees and/or subcommittees. Standing committees may include a membership committee, in charge of getting new members and sustaining the ones who have already joined, a program committee, and a special projects committee. Subcommittees or ad hoc committees are often established by the standing committees to help out with a project or special task. For example, the membership committee may appoint two subcommittees, one for new members, the other for sustaining members.

Fundraising Friends groups often publish a newsletter to circulate to members. This newsletter, undertaken by someone appointed to be in charge of publicity, makes certain that members know about the library's needs and know what needs have been met.

Fundraising groups are usually the most attractive to any type library because funds are usually so desperately needed. It isn't that fundraising groups are necessarily the best type of Friends groups. On the contrary, many public relations Friends groups have raised just as much money while having a different focus. But many financially strapped libraries find the directed efforts of a fundraising Friends group hard to resist.

These five major areas—fundraising, volunteer services, library awareness or literacy, public relations, and advocacy—do not constitute an exhaustive list of the areas in which Friends groups organize. But they are the major areas and indicate just how varied the Friends experience may be. While this book focuses mainly on fundraising groups, the principles and practices discussed can easily be applied to any Friends group.

Friends organizers need not focus on one purpose entirely! You may wish to combine several of the purposes listed above. The important thing to remember is that the limitations are placed on the group by you and others, not by anything inherent in the Friends process itself. The same may be said about the type of activities your group may undertake.

Friends' programs or activities are generally defined by the program committee, as well as by the group's constitution and by-laws and the demands placed on the Friends group by the administration (another reason why the group must be constituted with representative members from all concerned areas). Listed below are some of the many activities in which Friends groups participate:

- Book sales
- Rummage sales
- Auctions
- Luncheons
- Antique shows
- Teas
- Author autograph parties
- Sponsorship of endowed funds
- Sponsorship of special collections
- Special events and receptions
- Library birthday parties/anniversaries
- Book and coffee events
- Rare book displays
- Music recitals
- Dramatic performances or readings
- Special purchase sponsorship
- Annual library tours (field trips in the U.S. or abroad)
- Direct mailings
- Car washes
- Recycling events
- Sales activities (cards, cakes, bulbs, pizzas, etc.)

The Friends process may appear overwhelming at this point: mission, vision, purpose, officers, committees, subcommittees. How do you make sense of all this? *You* don't! It is now time to bring together a committee of interested members for the sole purpose of making some sense out of the process.

You are a leader with a vision and a mission. You now have some idea of the types and purposes of Friends groups. But you need to bring together a group of people representative of the library and the larger community to establish more firmly what kind of group you will form, its purpose, and the kinds of activities it will undertake. Now are you ready to begin? Perhaps a little soul-searching is in order first.

# SOUL-SEARCHING

A Friends group is fun and exciting, but it can also be hard work, not to mention a source of frustration for the person charged with organizing it. When contemplating whether or not to organize a Friends group, you must begin by asking yourself if you are willing to pay the price of hard work, after-hours planning, and the usual blood, sweat, and tears.

Your most important role as possessor of the vision and the mission of starting a Friends groups will be to develop a group of responsible individuals who will share your enthusiasm *and* your drive to see the group succeed. For example, the main reason why libraries have Friends groups is for support.[3] If the primary reason for setting up a Friends group is not support for the library, then it should not be undertaken.

Support here, as we have seen, extends beyond mere financial assistance to more philosophical support for the library and the totality of its functions. In this family of functions are included the genus culture and the species literacy. Library Friends groups ". . . create and stimulate public support of library programs . . . interpret the library to the community . . . encourage gifts to the library . . . [and] provide financial support beyond the library budget capacity."[4] When organizing your Friends group, you will want to look for people who can share in this vision of library service.

An easy mistake to make at this point would be for a library director or library staff member to say, "Since I already have that vision, why shouldn't I also be the Friends executive director?" Of course, you may serve in that role in order to *begin* the organization, but if the organization is to endure, you cannot *remain* that person indefinitely. Librarians involved with Friends groups in small libraries and small communities will act as Friends executive directors for longer periods of time than those who serve larger institutions in larger communities. More will be said about the director as "chief cook and bottle-washer" at a later time. For now, bear in mind that if you design the Friends group with yourself solidly at the helm, you will almost certainly see it die when your career calls you to move on.

But Friends groups *do* require an animating spirit to lead them to organization, and that is where you come in. Friends groups need an individual who will find equally energetic people to lead the organization. You, as the initial organizer of the group, should move to the background once the group is up and running. For now, the group needs your energy to find the right people.

It is important that the Friends group have at least some reverence, whether earnest or symbolic, for reading. For all their sophistication, libraries are still primarily about the business of reading and culture, to paraphrase Matthew Arnold. The person in charge of spearheading the Friends group should be committed to "... aid[ing] the Divine gift of language and letters to outlive us all," as Chesterton so aptly said.[5]

The Friends group will be filling a need and getting a return. In thinking about the mission and vision of your group, you will want to keep in mind the purpose of your library and the mission given it by your college or university administration, or by your Board of Trustees. The mission of the library, whether public or academic, will have a significant impact on the focus of your Friends group. The Friends group isn't the "pet" of the library. In fact, such groups in large academic or public libraries can become entirely independent of them. But what the Friends group is all about should be consistent with the mission of the library it is supporting.

The point is, in much the same way that the author of a short story must know what he or she wants to accomplish in a story and then devise the plot accordingly, the librarian setting up a Friends group must know the purpose of the group in order to design an appropriate course of action. Unfortunately, no matter what type of Friends group it is, the work is the same. Murphy's Law is in effect here, so it's going to take all the time you have and probably more. A Friends group of three dozen or three thousand requires the same amount of work; only the so-called "clerical" work increases as the membership enlarges.

As you begin the process of organizing a Friends organization, bear in mind that Friends groups take more than spare time to organize and sustain. In the Friends group I initiated, my staff of five and I worked on the Friends programs year-round. Of course, the work in the "off" months was never very taxing. But from six months before the dinner we held each fall until the event itself, the work increased almost exponentially. As head, or chief initiator or overseer, of the Friends group, you have to want it to work and have to want to invest the time to make it work.

Later on, when elections are held to place that special person in the office of president, your level of involvement will decrease. In the examples given earlier (from larger academic libraries), library directors and staffs spend very little of their time (10 percent or less) in direct involvement with their Friends organizations. In smaller academic or public libraries, the amount of director/staff time involved is often more than twice as much. In any case, the organizing of the group will require considerably more director/staff time and effort than the later stages. It is good to know this ahead of time so that you are not compelled to cancel your group for lack of time in the initial stages.

# ADDITIONAL CONSIDERATIONS

Is the director of the library fully committed to a successful Friends program? The ideal Friends group is one in which the library director is involved from the beginning, and then later, after the group is running smoothly, about five to ten percent of the time. But this is the ideal. Librarians wishing to organize a Friends group at a small library may have to undertake the organizer's role in addition to their staff position. It is difficult, if not impossible, to direct a successful Friends program if the library director is a reluctant player. Too many of the group's day-to-day operations require that the individual with the most intimate knowledge of the organization speak about it. This can involve speaking to anywhere from one or two members of the Friends group to several hundred. It may be possible to recruit members of the Friends group to serve as spokepersons for the library, but initially you will undoubtedly need to have the director involved—and in no small measure.

So important is this business of an interested library director that it is the first of ten commandments listed in the *Friends of Libraries Sourcebook*.[6] In fact, if the director is uninterested, you should probably forget the enterprise and organize your Friends group when you become director, or when your library gets a more willing director. Obviously this goes back to the willingness to invest the time.

Finally, do you have a problem with "closing the deal," as sales people are fond of saying? A good Friends organizer will not only seek out those with money (or public relations skills, or whatever), but will have no shyness in asking for whatever is needed.

Once you have answered these questions to your own satisfaction, you are ready to move on to the next step. A word of advice may be in order here. Commitment to the Friends group is essential to success. You simply cannot go into this relationship with the idea that it is something you can do in your spare time. Nor is it something you will be able to delegate away.

Seeing to success may mean that the strong leader will have to fill in the gaps that occur if things begin to falter. When frustration mounts, when the person assigned a job has fallen down on it, there has to be someone who will pick up the pieces, massage egos, run interference, and do whatever else needs to be done. That one person ought to be the person who has the vision and mission for the group. This means that the buck will always stop with you.

# THINGS TO DO

1. Collect articles and books on Friends groups and read them before going any further. The citations given in this book and in standard indexes should provide a good starting point. Sandy Dolnick's book *Friends of Libraries Sourcebook* is a particularly helpful resource.

2. Contact the Friends of Libraries USA. This very helpful organization will provide a wealth of materials and ideas upon which to ruminate. The address is:

   FOLUSA
   c/o American Library Association
   50 East Huron Street
   Chicago, IL 60611

   Be sure to see their book, *Friends of the Library National Notebook*.

3. Call a Friends of the Library group in your area (the Friends of Libraries USA group mentioned above can help you locate other groups in your area). It will not matter if you talk with an academic, public, or special library Friends organizer, since the advice is adaptable. Talk with the person directly involved in the group, but don't stop there. Ask if you can come to a meeting. If possible, call a few regular members.

4. Draw up a mock program for a Friends group. It may not be the best thing you've done, but it will give you some idea of the mind power needed to get one going.

5. Examine your library's history and see if there is anything unique about it that would provide you with a good rallying point for a first meeting.

# ENDNOTES

1. Ronnelle K.H. Thompson, *Friends of College Libraries (CLIP Note #9)*.
2. See also Sandy Dolnick (ed.), *Friends of Libraries Sourcebook*, 2d ed., p.1.
3. See E. Holley, "The Library and Its Friends" in *Organizing the Library's Support*, edited by D.W. Krummel.
4. Ann G. Matthews, "The Library Friends and Regional Library Networks" in *Organizing the Library's Support*, edited by D. W. Krummel, p. 41.
5. G.K. Chesterton, *G.K.C. as M.C. Being a Collection of Thirty-Seven Introductions*. Selected and edited by J.P. de Fonseka. London: Methuen & Co. Ltd., 1929, p. 223.
6. Dolnick, *Friends of Libraries Sourcebook*, 2d ed., p. 3.

# ORGANIZING THE STEERING COMMITTEE

So, you have decided to organize a Friends of the Library group. You and your library staff have discussed the idea with the appropriate administrative staff, including your director and Board of Trustees, or university officials, and have determined that such an organization is tenable. Where do you go from here? The next step involves putting together a steering committee. You might think that all you need to do is get a few names together, call them up, and, presto! You have the committee! Would that it were so easy. Some groups, no doubt, have organized without proceeding in the methodical manner described below. But the survival rate of those groups is, no doubt, quite low.

Before bringing together the steering committee, you should give some thought to the decision-making framework or system that the committee will use. Perhaps this will strike some readers as superfluous. They might think, "I am already in the process of making decisions." That may well be so. But the question is whether the form of decision-making you currently use is the best for beginning a Friends group.

This chapter discusses the importance of participative decision making and early establishment of goals and objectives as they relate to the Friends steering committee.

## SHARED DECISION MAKING AND STAFF RELATIONS

Shared decision making (or participative decision making as it is called in professional circles) is the best mode of decision making to be followed in a Friends group. This is not because it renders the best decisions. In fact, research tells us that it sometimes does not. But it does render decisions that are implemented. Members who have shared in the decision-making process are far more likely to implement decisions arising out of that context than those that have been ordered to do so.

Bear in mind that you are seeking to create an organization that will be self-perpetuating. If you begin this process by making all the decisions yourself, what will happen when you leave, or if you cannot get followers to "buy into" your ideas? In a small town, you may have trouble finding outside volunteers, but remember: A

Friends group that relies on only one person is destined for the dustbin as soon as that person leaves town, burns out, or retires.

## BOTTOM-UP VERSUS TOP-DOWN

All too often, managers, whether they are librarians or not, think that once *they* have decided a matter, it's time for everyone else to move. When the decision concerns the start-up of a Friends of the Library program, you cannot do the task alone, but you cannot demand that everything be done by others who have not participated in the decision-making process either. You need help, and that help must come from a variety of sources: local leadership, your staff, and your community. In order to secure the help of these various groups, a decision-making process that allows for participation in decisions of all interested members is imperative. Not everyone will, of course, participate in the decision-making process, but that is *their* decision to make. You have to provide a framework for decision making that will allow anyone who wants to participate to do so. Participative management does just that.

It is interesting to note that participative decision making, or PDM, is often talked about, even raved about evangelically, but practiced very little. A survey of library directors by Victoria Kline Musman reported in *California Librarian* revealed, not too surprisingly, that many of them thought of themselves as participative managers. Then she did something for which she shall forever do penance: She asked the *staffs* of those same directors what management style was used by their fearless leaders. Overwhelmingly, those staffs said, "authoritative."[1]

## PDM DEFINED

What is participative (or shared) decision making? It is not a matter of making up one's mind and then telling others to carry it out. Nor is it a matter of making up one's mind and then asking others what they think. It is not even a matter of making up one's mind and then finding out how others feel about it, making adjustments, and then presenting it as the last word on the matter.

True participative management is a "mode of organizational operation in which decisions as to activities are arrived at by the very persons who are to execute those decisions."[2] Participative decision making is that style of management in which "subordinates and superordinates work together as equals rather than in an hierarchical arrangement."[3] But there are, as we shall see, other levels of participative decision making. It is important to find one aspect of it that relates best to your circumstances.

## FALSE IMAGES

Participative decision making conjures up two images almost at once. The first is one that takes the leader off the hook. "Participation?" the manager says, "Oh, yeah, that. I do that. I let my staff talk about my decisions every two weeks." This is not participative decision making any more than a faculty meeting called by the president of a college with an agenda set by the dean is. PDM is much more than this.

The second image is far more dramatic and, perhaps, far more damaging to the true participative decision making arrangement. When the phrase "participative decision making" is uttered, groans issue from the lips of leaders, accompanied by the lament, "There goes my power." Their minds may be flooded with images like the storming of the Bastille and Louis XVI being carried off to the guillotine. Turning over all decision-making power to the staff is not PDM either.

Leaders cannot function without power. PDM is not a means whereby power is abdicated, either partially or completely. It is a process wherein power is *shared*.

Friends organizers need to understand that successful groups are those in which power is shared. There is, however, still one place where the buck stops. John Calvin, the great Protestant reformer, once said that in every relationship, someone must lead. Participative decision making does not mean—one may go so far as to say it never means—forgetting this rule of thumb. But the leadership formula for success is never, or should never be, that the leader always says "x" and the followers always do it.

## SHARING POWER

The question of management or leadership has been raised because Friends groups cannot be mandated. First of all, you are trying to organize a *group*, not a one-person show. This has been stressed before but needs to be underscored again and again. If nothing else, common courtesy tells us that the people who are to be most affected by a given decision need to be consulted first. If they are ignored entirely, the result is likely to be disastrous, especially for a people-focused activity like a Friends of the Library program.

Recall for a moment the definition given earlier of participative decision making: ". . . subordinates and superordinates work[ing] together as equals. . . ." This is what a Friends group is all about.

Groups form and have an impact on organizational development and climate. Heads of Friends of the Library organizations must ask themselves how they can structure those groups for optimal gain and then work to achieve that effect. If you want to influence the group process for success, participative decision making is probably the best approach.

## CHECKING STAFF TEMPERATURES

How do you tell if your staff is ready to undertake this enterprise known as a Friends group? Sure, many staff members may readily agree that a Friends group is a great idea. Those same people may also be relying on someone else to do the work! In order to avoid misjudgment, a good place to begin is with job descriptions. If a previous director has been sagacious enough to include such an activity in the job description, this will help, but it will not be "all there is," especially if there has been no Friends group in recent memory. For small libraries, this is a good idea anyway. Chances are there is neither a job description nor a job manual for staff in small libraries. You can begin to build your Friends group by creating the job descriptions and the job manual in collaboration with other staff members.

The second thing that can be done is to watch staff member behaviors. See how they respond to extra work, whether they take it upon themselves to engage in extra work, and how efficaciously that work is performed. If staff members are reluctant to do anything that is not "in my job description," chances are they will not be very open to additional work created by Friends activities. Further, a staff member who does extra activities but does them poorly will probably be useful to you and the Friends group only on limited and highly supervised assignments. Poor, ineffectual, or discourteous work will sink a Friends' flagship before it leaves port.

## CHECKING RESUMES

The wise librarian seeking to organize a Friends group will examine the resumes of staff members for clues about activities that might be appropriate to the Friends enterprise. Are certain staff members active in other civic organizations? Are they good with publicity? Do they make a good impression on people? Are they good at communicating and meeting others? All of these clues will help you to plan and organize this group effectively.

Of course you should meet with staff members, but as a final episode in this prelude of preparation. Friends organizers are in very delicate positions. Think about it. A director calls a special meeting and, trying to put on the most open face possible, ends up asking for "volunteers." A bright and enthusiastic Friends librarian wants to meet with those who might be interested in helping with such a group, and everyone immediately says "No, I'm too busy already." The Friends organizers who have done their homework will find that these problems can be circumvented. Zero in on the strengths and weaknesses of individual members in order to make sure you outfit your flagship with the appropriate "sailors."

# COMMUNICATION AND FRIENDS GROUPS

Communication is a key element in the formation of Friends groups, not to mention their survival. You have now communicated with staff, but that is only the beginning. Communication is essential, not only for the library staff, or the executive head who will lead the larger membership, but for each member. If a Friends groups is going to be successful, it *must* have communication, and it must have it regularly. Nothing kills a newly formed Friends group faster than silence.

In addition to communication, Friends groups should also exhibit purposiveness, interdependence, group distinctiveness and a desire for success.[4] Purposiveness will come as the steering committee forms and sets goals. Interdependence implies a mutually supportive relationship between the Friends group and the library. Group distinctiveness is an evolutionary process that develops with age. Distinctiveness comes from the group itself, from the personalities of individual members. Group distinctiveness also develops out of the steering committee's study of community needs and desires. Groups need to come together and decide what it is that is going to make them different from all other groups. It must be a mix of the ordinary and the extraordinary.

## COMMUNITY READINESS

It is now time to get a barometer reading on the community. This will be familiar to public librarians, less so to their academic counterparts. It will do no good to get the Friends steering committee together and get it all dressed up if there is positively no place for it to go. What does the community like? What events do its members respond to? What activities in the community produce at least a break-even return for organizations sponsoring them? These are questions that must be answered. It will help if a Friends group can get these answers before sponsoring events that are doomed to failure.

The librarian in search of a Friends group may already be a member of several civic groups. Some may consider such memberships a waste of time, but to the academic or public library Friends organizer they are essential. The hands-on experience, the successes and the failures, of these civic groups can help the Friends organizer immeasurably. They can also be an invaluable resource for identifying potential members—and leaders—for your steering committee.

Begin to search out your community and its potential leaders by making a list of all the organizations in the community. Such a list, if you cannot compile one, will most likely be available through the local chamber of commerce. If a chamber is not functioning in the city, a check with the city or town hall should supply this information.

It will be necessary for the Friends steering committee to have on hand the names of these civic organizations, their presidents, and their club meeting times. It would also be helpful to find out what kinds of activities they provide for the community each year. For example, the Lion's Club may sponsor a few paper drives or a broom and mop sale. This kind of information is important because it tells the Friends steering committee what kind of event *not* to plan. You don't want to compete with anyone if you can help it. You want to carve your own special niche for your group.

Any printed matter these groups have to share will also help you, including any organizing materials such as by-laws and constitutions. Asking for samples will be a big help to your first organizational meeting. The more information you have on hand, the more likely you will be able to convince those who come on board of the seriousness of your enterprise.

## WHY BUILDING RELATIONSHIPS IS IMPORTANT

What you are trying to do is build a relationship that isn't entirely superficial. You want be known to the media, civic leaders, and other community influentials. Why is this so important? Because whatever the relative value of the friendship you are able to develop, each person you meet during this process represents at least one potential Friends member. If the truth be told, however, most community leaders represent many more than one potential Friends member. Even if only half of these contacts ever attend a Friends function, they are, nevertheless, influential in the community. What they say and think *matters*, not only to you, but also to the community at large. Make one or two of them mad, and you'll see in an instant how much influence they have. It isn't that bad news travels faster than good, it's just that it wreaks more havoc along the way.

## TIME IS OF THE ESSENCE

If you are a new library employee and have the task of developing a Friends group, strengthening these relationships will take no less than nine months to a year. You can, of course, make friends faster than that. But they will be ephemeral friendships, ones that will not be sustainable over the years. What you must do is get out in the community and be seen as someone they can trust, someone who contributes to, not just takes from, the community. This means understanding what the community is about and what it means to be a member of Whatever Town, USA. Doing this means meeting lots of people and talking with them about the town's history, politics, religions, and *raison d'etre*. Doing *that* takes time, and lots of it.

## GETTING ADVICE

Once you have established yourself in the community and have made several calls on some of the civic organizations, you are ready to make the rounds of those groups and ask for advice. The advice does not have to be specific: "Our library staff is thinking about starting a Friends group and wanted to see how your group got started and what it has been doing." You could approach it as someone who is interested in what they are doing, organizationally, especially. Be sure to take notes, for you will find out many names of individuals you will want to try to meet later. Gather together every piece of evidence in paper form that you can find from these groups and try to adapt their successes to your Friends group. Remember that your task—should you choose to accept it—is to begin a successful program, not reinvent the wheel. If you are a member in several of these organizations, and have even served on their boards in some capacity, so much the better.

## ESTABLISHING AN ADDRESS FILE

Friends organizers need to begin as soon as possible to establish an address file for potential contacts. This list should include not only names of individuals who are involved in the community, but also potential contributors. For Friends of academic libraries, organizers should begin with the development office and continue to work with this office throughout the life of the organization. Failure to do so may embarrass not only you, but the entire academic community.

For Friends of public libraries, a list of *former* library trustees is a good place to begin. Former trustees are stressed here because it muddles matters too much to have a current trustee also serve as a member of the Board of Friends. Current trustees can join the Friends group, but it is best not to make them organizational members also. Public library Friends organizers will also want to review the list of frequent users of their libraries. Some discernment is needed here. Checking out any number of library materials each week does not automatically qualify someone as a potential Friends member. Look at the whole picture of library usage, then decide on whose support to enlist.

## FLYERS

Putting up flyers in the library is also helpful, especially if you make them just mysterious enough to arouse curiosity and provoke questions. You might want to place a small ad in the local paper and put other flyers around town in strategic places, or wherever "bookish" culture is likely to be highly esteemed. The idea is that when you put together the steering committee, you want to be sure you have individuals who are passionately interested in this enterprise.

# STUDYING THE COMMUNITY

We have already seen how the Friends organizer can tap the resources of existing civic groups. But how do you go about *studying* the community? As indicated earlier, public librarians will be familiar with this process, but academic librarians may need more detailed direction.

One very effective way to study the community is to glean clues from a variety of local sources. Attend a few functions in town in order to see who else attends. Pay attention to the programming on local television stations, which is often tailored to the interests of the community. Note the content of the local newspaper. (The news section of our northeastern Tennessee community paper was a total of six pages, while the sports section was usually about 20!) You need this kind of information before the steering committee meets because you want to be able to supply them with information that will help them to make good decisions. For example, providing your steering committee with the knowledge that your community of 15,000 turns out for Friday night football games in the thousands will help them eliminate Friday night for the Friends group's activities.

Most communities operate in a general environment that includes three aspects: social, economic, and political.[5] Your community study should examine all three aspects. If you do not plan with these in mind, you may wind up with a good program and no audience.

## THE SOCIAL ASPECT

The social aspect includes such things as what the community likes, what it dislikes, what it will tolerate, what it will not, and what it will support fully. It also includes things like the local papers and radio and television stations. Their support is of essential importance to your program. Involving them early on will serve you well later. You must *plan* to involve them by contacting them and talking with them about their needs as well as your own. Public library Friends organizers should attempt to get a media representative to serve on their steering committee. While the same is true of organizers for Friends of academic libraries, other people more immediately influential may have to be put in place on that steering committee first.

Two things need to be kept in mind at all times. One, you do not want the steering committee to be too big. Two, for the type of library you work in, you need to make certain that all constituents are represented, not only on the steering committee, but also on the executive board of the Friends organization. The number of constituent groups that must be represented will help determine the number of members of both boards. Because colleges and universities can be private enterprises, media representatives, while important, may have to give way to donors, alumni, students, faculty, and the administration.

## THE ECONOMIC ASPECT

The economic condition of the community should also be considered. If the Friends organizer wants to have a real show-stopper of an event, then he or she must take into consideration whether or not the community is able to support it. Small communities will surprise, both in what they like and what they will support—two distinctively different things. The simple fact of being small does not mean that the community is economically insufficient. But scheduling events that are costly for those living in depressed economic areas will lead to a large overhead and a small, if not nonexistent, profit.

## THE POLITICAL ASPECT

Lastly, the political element in your general environment is very important to know. Many Friends programs have sunk because the Friends organizer did not pay any attention to community politics. Getting a political reading on a community can help immensely in planning program events. If one knows ahead of time, for example, that the community is essentially apolitical, having a well-known political pundit to speak at a dinner program or annual event will probably not bring much success. Though an idea might seem potentially earthshaking on paper, hosting it without understanding the political interests of the community will only result in frustration and possible failure. By the same token, if you invite a political figure whose ideas are directly opposite those of most members of your community, the end result will probably be a town full of enemies for the Friends program director. This kind of insensitivity will also hurt the rest of the environment in which the Friends group functions.

With academic and special libraries, there are other "environments" to consider. For example, academic settings tend to produce an immediate community that maintains more left-leaning views than the community at large.[6] Planning events based solely on what *that* community likes may well alienate the Friends organization from the rest of the community. This kind of misstep will only ensure that the program will never reach beyond the limits of the academic community to which it is tied.

Organizers of Friends groups for public libraries are only too aware of the political ramifications of their work in the community. Because public libraries are tax-driven institutions, every taxpaying citizen is your boss. Ignoring the political ramifications of this relationship will spell certain trouble. Organizers of public library Friends groups will therefore want to include as many "power-brokers" in the steering committee as possible. This might include former council members, PTO and PTA members and other individuals involved in education, media representatives, and the community's "movers and shakers."

## TALK WITH POWER BROKERS

It is also important to talk with the "power brokers" in the community. How to identify these brokers will be discussed at length in chapter 3. Suffice it for now to say that asking these people about their interests, the history of civic participation in the region, and the kinds of events that might have a good turnout will help the Friends organizer hit upon the right combination. Of course, one can also try a hit-or-miss strategy, but beginning with one or two failures will do nothing to build internal morale. If some staff members are reluctant but nevertheless willing to help, one or two failures may fuel the fire of discontent enough to cost you some supporters.

Other places to go for good background data include standard reference sources such as census reports and market guides. These will help the Friends librarian put together materials that will assist him or her later in structuring financially productive programs. In other words, you are trying to build group distinctiveness, a point that cannot be stressed too much. *If the Friends group is going to succeed, it cannot duplicate the work of other groups or provide something so dramatically different as to place itself outside the market. It must position itself within the community, fulfilling a specific need.* This can only be done after some study has been conducted to see what the waters are like.

# THE FRIENDS STEERING COMMITTEE

The steering committee for a Friends group in an academic setting should be made up of the library director, one or two interested staff members, a member of the administration, one or two faculty members, one or two student members, some alumni, and several interested college or university patrons from the community. For the public library setting, the committee might include one or two former trustees, the library director, the head of the PTO or PTA, a council member (active or otherwise), a current or former head of one or two civic organizations (e.g., Lion's Club or Rotary Club) and key media individuals. The media individuals do not have to be newspaper or television personalities, but may be individuals who have had success working with those outlets.

The names you have gathered from the process described above will provide you with plenty of names from which to select. In the case of academic Friends groups, before you ask anyone from the community to serve, check your list of names with the development office of your college or university to be sure you are not stealing someone away from another program. It's easy to step on toes, especially ones the development office may already be standing on, so be sure to check first.

The steering committee will determine the purpose of your Friends group by examining the needs of the library, its overall mission, the mission of the university or college, if academic, or the mission and purpose of your public library. This group will need to decide such matters as what the Friends group will focus on and how that focus will tie into the library's overall goals, the college or university's mission, or the servicing of public library needs. The need for wide representation is quite obvious. For example, a college administration might like the Friends group to act as another arm of the overall public relations effort. A public relations Friends group would then become the chief organizing principle. The trustees of a public library might want to stress literacy, so a literacy Friends group would be in order. But let committee members decide this. Whatever you do, don't be in too big of a hurry to bring this group to closure without adequate discussion from all the represented groups.

Once this group has determined the type of Friends group it would like to be, it should begin thinking about the recruitment of a strong Friends director. This may be a paid or unpaid position, depending on how the academic administration or public library board of trustees wants the group structured. Even if the group is to be entirely independent of the library, you will still want to discuss with the college administration or board of trustees what the group can or should do for the library. Establishing cross-purposes this early on in the development of the Friends group could result in the group's eventual demise.

Most Friends directors are lay leaders, so you will want to scout out that "perfect" person to be your Friends leader. You will find this person by using your steering committee as a sounding board. Ask members from this group to submit names and reasons for submitting them. Then have the group examine the "resume" of each member offered. Selection will eventually be made based on what is best for the Friends organization.

*Make haste slowly*, as the saying goes, with this selection. This person will be the chief animator for the group. A hasty decision regarding this person may well spell defeat for the group later. If any one person is essential for a Friends group it is a Friends director with the passion and energy to bring the group into focus. Some may think that the best approach is to wait and have this person elected by the small membership at an initial meeting of the Friends group. But this person is too important to leave his or her selection to chance, or to the forces of popularity. Subsequent elections will, of course, determine the president or executive director of the group. But your group *must* begin with as near-perfect a person as can be found. That person will serve as an example for the subsequent presidents or executive directors your group will need to elect.

Steering committee members should also begin thinking of programs that the Friends group might want to undertake. At this point you will want to offer the committee the community study you have done. Obviously, a program committee will be appointed later. But some idea of what programs will work in your community will need to be examined. These will be evident from your community study.

# INITIATING AN ACTION PLAN: OBJECTIVES

The steering committee will also want to think in terms of objectives. Some of these will be dictated by the purpose of the Friends group. The committee begins a plan of action by identifying objectives. Objectives are the means to goals. Objectives will be added as the organization grows to reflect better those that make up its membership. But for now, the Friends steering committee must come up with a handful of objectives that the organization will want to achieve immediately. These objectives should be both short-term and long-term in nature. They can also be of any variety: economic, social, or political. These objectives will by necessity be general in nature.

## OBJECTIVES=RESULTS

The purpose of these objectives is to get the organization from the cerebral, intellectual stages, to the actual, action-oriented ones. It is important that these objectives be ones that anyone can understand, and that they be tied to a specific action.

For example, one objective of virtually any Friends group should be longevity, endurance, sustaining power—in a word, survival. This at once becomes a plan of action. The Friends steering committee asks itself, "What do we need to do in order to survive?" There should follow a number of other activities that then become subobjectives. This will create a web or a network of "things to do" and will create enough work to keep a dozen or more people working. Survival, for example, would bring up the necessity of recruiting members, since no one can do these things alone. It would also bring up the maddening issue of funding and ways to achieve it. And, it would further necessitate the writing of a constitution and by-laws. From one objective, four or five activities emerge that can then be planned and implemented.

# CHECKPOINT

At this point, a checklist might be helpful to indicate where you are in this organizing process:

1. You have determined that a Friends groups needs to be organized. Staff have been consulted and are agreeable to investigating the idea. The Friends group has the blessings *and* the involvement of the library director.

2. Appropriate people have been invited to a "draft a Friends group" meeting. This group includes members of the library staff, representatives of the administration, faculty, students, and perhaps one or two lay people. It also might include former trustees, media representatives, civic club members, and lay leaders. In the case of a public library, the guest list should include one or two former trustees, the library director, one or two staff members, patrons of the library whose usage indicates a strong interest, one or two members of civic groups, and one or two media representatives. This nucleus of people will be your steering committee.

3. The steering committee has determined the purpose of the Friends group (i.e., public relations, volunteers, fundraising, or other).

4. The steering committee discusses possible leaders who could act as the Friends director.

5. The library director (or some library staff member) has made a community study to determine the social, economic, and political aspects of the community. These are reported to the Friends steering committee.

6. The Friends steering committee discusses objectives of the group and makes certain these objectives relate to goals.

# THINGS TO DO

1. Visit your local chamber of commerce's director or president. Ask for a list of civic groups and their contact persons. While visiting with the director, also ask for a list of community events and actual community participation rates. Perhaps your community has had an "Autumn Chase" event or a "Summerfest" gathering. What was done, and how well was it attended? You might want to make a grid like the one below:

| Event | Group Responsible | Attendance | Outcome |
|---|---|---|---|
| Festival | Lion's Club | 2,000 | + $40 |
| Autumn Chase | Rotary, Civitans | 4,000 | -$1,600 |

By placing it on a chart, you are more likely to get a better "feel" for what went right and what did not.

2. Visit with coordinators of events you identified. Talk over what they did and how they went about doing it.

3. Check with the local television or radio station managers. What programs are the ones most watched or listened to? Ask the managers why they think this is so.

4. Review your staff's reactions to the assignment of extra duties. Were they willing and able to execute these assigned duties competently? A chart or grid of duties that have been assigned through the years will bring the pertinent information to the foreground quickly for Friends group use:

| Employee | Activity | Accomplishment | Recommendation |
|---|---|---|---|
| Bob | Book sale | Failed to show | Not suited |
| Cindy | Inventory | Took charge | Excellent |

Were you happy with the work? Who emerges as the "natural" leader in these events? Do you see any patterns developing that would dovetail nicely with the Friends group?

5. How would you rate your staff's ability to deal with change and conflict? Do they "rally together" well, or is there an every-man-for-himself attitude?

6. Make a list of five or six activities and ask several people who have lived in the area longer than you have whether they would attend such an event or not. Be sure to ask them why they would or would not attend.

7. Ask several people on your campus or in the community to serve as a nucleus for the steering committee. If you're in an academic setting, make sure you get representation from the administration, the faculty, students, and alumni. Leaders will come from suggestions from this nucleus, and from your "spade work" with civic groups. If you're in a public library, seek representatives from key civic groups, parent or school organizations, political circles, and others that represent the diverse segments of your community.

# ENDNOTES

1. Victoria Kline Musman, "Managerial Style in a Small Public Library," *California Librarian*, July 1978: 7-20.
2. Aaron Lowin. "Participative Decision Making: A Model, Literature Critique, and Prescriptions for Research," *Organizational Behavior and Human Performance* 3: 69.
3. C.J. Wood, "Participatory Decision Making: Why Doesn't It Seem To Work," *Educational Forum* 49: 55.
4. See A. Zander, *Making Groups Effective*, p. 2-9. This book is an excellent guide to successful participative decision making.
5. R.L. Daft, *Organization Theory and Design*.
6. For more thorough treatments of this topic, see D. D'Souza, *Illiberal Education*; Seymour Lipsett, "The Academic Mind at the Top," *Public Opinion Quarterly* 46: 143-168; and S. Rothman, "Academics on the Left," *Society* 23, No. 3: 4-8.

# 3 PLANNING FOR ACTION

With the steering committee now in place and a framework set for decision making that will include all members who wish to participate, a few words about planning are in order. Without some conscious effort made at planning, important tasks, however democratically arranged, may not be implemented in an orderly fashion. Planning is the key step that must be taken to make certain that tasks assigned are in fact carried out.

## PLANNING DEFINED

Planning involves three essential steps. The first step is to identify distinct tasks that must be done in order to achieve objectives. For example, in planning for the kickoff meeting for the Friends group, certain tasks must be done: workers must be lined up; a meeting place obtained; an agenda developed; announcements or invitations sent out; and refreshments, if desired, arranged.

The second step is *assignment* of responsibility—carrying out those tasks. Assignments should be given to each member of a given committee. Members must know what they are to do. It is a good idea to tell each person orally, and to provide each with a written list of designated responsibilities.

Finally, the third step is setting *deadlines* for completing each task. Members need to know what to do, but they must also have a "day of reckoning," or a day when they must say whether they did or did not get the task done and why. Of all the steps, the setting of deadlines is probably the most frequently omitted in the planning process. Yet, this is the part of the planning process by which one is able to *make certain that the plan has been executed*.

## SUCCESSFUL PLANS = ACTION

What makes a successful plan? Action. Note the word carefully. It is not a dustbin-of-history plan, or a plan to occupy space on a page and not to occupy the thoughts of anyone else. It must be carefully worked out. This does not mean that it is so complex that a copy of it must always be nearby. But major points must not be left open-ended: "Someone will arrange a meeting pretty soon after we're organized, whenever that will be."

Though the production of a plan for organization may be the work of only three or four people, it must not ignore the existence of others who are or will be involved in the organization later. In other words, leave room for growth so that it will not take a board decision to override the simplest of procedures.

## PLAN EVERYTHING

Planning must begin at the beginning, however obvious that may seem. Your plan should outline steps for early organizational development, the recruitment of executive leadership of the Steering Committee, as well as the recruitment of the membership of the group itself, and general statements covering the areas of responsibility for each group. For example, if you have in mind that the steering committee should appoint a task force to study possible community leaders for the Friends group, then you should write that down as one of the steering committee's goals. It cannot be left to chance. Planning that is not present at creation, so to speak, will only serve as an inadequate "Band-Aid" solution to the many problems that will inevitably arise later. Planning, like reading, is fundamental.

## DON'T REINVENT THE WHEEL

While what works for one Friends group will not always work for another, you don't want to reinvent the wheel. Even though it is hard to adapt a plan for one group by overlaying it on another, examine the planning procedures of other successful organizations, including other successful Friends groups. Friends of Libraries USA (FOLUSA) was created for just this purpose. Use it along with other professional contacts. Hints and clues could be garnered from these groups for future use.

## THE FOUR ELEMENTS OF ACTION PLANS

Action plans contain four ingredients: unity, continuity, flexibility, and accuracy. A word about each will help illustrate the importance of a good action plan.

Unity is what brings together the whole plan and guides it from one point to another. Unity helps prevent plans from becoming separated from the action that brings them to fruition, or from the objectives certain actions seek to obtain. It also helps to point out what needs to be done, either step-by-step or in a concurrent manner, so that actions will follow an orderly path. Unity of purpose helps to bring actions together under one heading.

Continuity of the action plan differs from unity in that continuity connects the smaller points of action together. Nothing undermines a group more quickly than the idea among followers that the leader doesn't know where the group is going. Continuity helps to eliminate this possibility. Continuity is that part of the plan that, to borrow teachers' lingo, keeps members on task. It also helps make certain that instead of alternative plans being undertaken by individuals with hidden agendas (not one of whom knows what the other is doing), there is one overarching plan that assures everyone that all are working along an orderly path toward the same objectives and, ultimately, the same goals.

Flexibility is the third aspect of a good plan. Publius, the great farceur, pointed this out centuries ago in one of his more serious moods: "Bad is the plan that can never be changed."

Flexibility is the saving grace of any plan. Without it, the plan will surely fail at some point. Some leaders have the mistaken impression that a plan is conceived and then followed slavishly, with deviations made only at the "deviant's" risk. Nothing could be further from the truth.

Flexibility allows for change and the addition of new information. Since Friends organizations are what is known as "open" systems (i.e., they do not function in a boundary closed to outside influences), they should always be receiving new information. The addition of this new information, be it economic, social, political, or internal, should have some effect on the Friends group, varying from slight to monumental. Flexibility in action plans allows for this new information to be added, and for adjustments to be made accordingly. Flexibility also helps to prevent instability from upsetting the Friends group.

Accuracy, the last item in good plans, must be viewed in a relative manner. Accuracy means that the plan is put together in conjunction with reality as it is perceived by those involved in the plan's preparation. Plans that have no place for accuracy are sprawling and disjointed with objectives that may or may not be reached in one year or 100 years. Accuracy means sticking to the facts as they are known at the time of the plan, by those most closely associated with the organization.

Obviously, flexibility will help stabilize plans and ensure their accuracy by correcting them when they are too far afield, or loosening them up when they are too tightly drawn. But the plan must be accurate in the context of the reality in which it is drawn.

The relativistic element mentioned here has to do with the timing of the plan, not the "quality of the accuracy."

## WARNINGS

No Friends steering committee can know everything. Regardless of its intentions, a committee may put together a plan for growth that is not accurate in some ways. Unfortunately, it is just this fact—the attitude that no plan can ever be fully accurate—that leads some Friends groups to map out plans that are entirely inaccurate. Objectives may be written in such a way that they cannot ever be accomplished in that community, or by the people involved in the group. Or, some objectives may be set that are totally inappropriate for the Friends group to which they are attached. A steering committee often can avoid useless plans simply by asking, "Is this an accurate assessment of our situation?"

## ACTION PLANS AND TIME

The single most common mistake Friends steering committees make in regard to planning is that they do not put a deadline on anything. Consequently, it is always in the process of *getting* done but is never completed. This is also true of group decision making. In the same way that a group needs a time limit to decide, so also does a Friends steering committee need a time limit by which things should be done.

Because Friends steering committees consist of humans, they often approach the task with a common ambivalence. Some will say, "Let it take all the time it needs." Other will argue that it should have been done yesterday. Time limits or deadlines should be attached to each part of the plan in order to make certain it is being carried out. If the plan is not scripted according to time, it will always be in a state of perpetual "almost."

## LONG-RANGE PLANS

Obviously, long-range plans will be developed by the Friends organization proper. But it is not improper for the Friends steering committee to think of the future. If the Friends group is to survive, a long-range plan that sketches possible outcomes will provide the executive committee with some idea of where the group began and where it wants to be in the future. The use of several plans tied together by a common purpose will help do that.

One-, three-, and six-month plans are recommended to set immediate priorities for a given year. An annual plan and a three-year plan can help in setting long-range objectives. Long-range plans are better designed by the permanent and ongoing Friends boards and contain more developmental objectives and goals.

## KEEP A RECORD

By now it should be obvious that any plan should be *written down*. There is an old belief among fiction writers that if you get a good idea for a story, don't tell it to anyone; write it first. The same could be said for plans. Plans that are only "thought up" are half-baked ideas and are not real plans. Plans have to be written down. The first attempt at this may yield only half a sheet of paper and may consist of things that seem painfully obvious. But the *act* of writing down the plan is essential because it teaches the planner how to plan. It is also the first step in accountability for the program.

# SAMPLE PLAN

What might a plan for the future of a Friends group look like at this point? The following sample provides a thumbnail sketch of the first steps you will take in forming a Friends of the Library group. The amount of time each step requires depends largely on your knowledge of the community, the number of people involved in its initialization, the level of interest, the amount of time people volunteer to the Friends effort, and the complexity of organization the group sets for itself (i.e., whether or not the group will seek formal incorporation as a separate, tax-exempt organization and how complex the internal organizational structure will be).

None of the steps below are etched in stone. The important point to remember is that you, along with other members who are discussing the Friends idea, have to decide what works best for the group, the library, and the community.

## FRIENDS PLAN OF ORGANIZATION

1. Recruit steering committee members (eight weeks).
2. Determine community needs (six weeks).
3. Determine who the power brokers are (ten weeks).
4. Build executive board (six weeks; names submitted from steering committee members and others).

5. Recruit Friends leader (names submitted from steering committee and executive board members).
6. Determine purpose or mission and goals of Friends group.
7. Review operations procedures (four weeks):
   a. Constitution
   b. By-Laws
   c. Membership fees.
8. Examine program potential for the area (eight weeks):
   a. Type
   b. Funding need
   c. Approaches to funding.

Now let's look at these areas one at a time and see what kind of information will be needed for each one.

# BUILDING THE EXECUTIVE BOARD

This can be a difficult task or an easy one. Whichever it is, it is by far the most serious or crucial activity in the early going. It isn't that this board is etched in stone, but its vitality often makes the difference between a successful or unsuccessful Friends group. These first few people will pass on their enthusiasm to the members who come on board later, both those who serve in the other offices of the Friends organization (on committees) and the membership at large.

While the steering committee can serve on the executive board, some members may not want to. At the same time, some members must carry on for the sake of continuity. Those that do become executive board members need to carry with them some notion of how to plan. Like its predecessor, the executive board should include new members representative of the academic community and the non-academic community, or of the public library community. But the potential members should also include more community members not wedded so closely to the public or academic library, or the college or university.

Executive board members must be selected carefully, not only for their ability to work within the group context but their ability to work with one another. Several personality traits surface as the most important. These are, in no real order of importance: commitment (to the Friends program), altruism, versatility, and creativity.

Commitment to the Friends program cannot, unfortunately, be measured by a paper and pencil test. This will be talked about in more detail in the next chapter. For now, it is important that something be known about each member. If the Friends organizer is new to the area, it will be necessary to wait at least a year before beginning the Friends program. This must be done in order to give that person time to learn about the community and who its workers are—that's just how important this selection process is. If members have worked with any group of people for very long, solicit advice from them about potential members. Perhaps in a different context, their work habits are known. Has someone worked with them on a committee in church or in a civic organization? Can someone else vouch for them?

Of course, this should be discussed with all the members of the steering committee. The steering committee, using its collective wisdom, should prepare a list of individuals that it definitely wants to ask to serve on the executive board.

In an academic setting, certain protocols will have to be observed. Of course, included on this list of possible executive board members will be *some* of the steering committee members. Other potential candidates might include past generous contributors to the library, members of various arts or symphony guilds, and members of other cultural and civic groups.

Friends of public libraries working through this process will also want to have some carryover from the steering committee. Other members might include past board presidents, retired librarians from the area, cultural and civic members, retired trustees, and the like. As with the building of the steering committee, *representation* is the key word.

Altruism in potential executive board members is also important. You are looking for people who want to see something done because it is worth doing. Someone who does not easily comprehend why a Friends group is important would not be a useful member. In looking for the truly altruistic, be discerning. The bluestocking lady may love to talk about literature, but can she sell tickets? The president of the Junior League may read every bestseller in your public library, but will she work hard?

Versatility is a key quality in potential board members. What is definitely *not* needed are those whose minds run along only one track, or whose minds run on only one track at a time. Sometimes these individuals can, inadvertently, derail a Friends group's enterprises. Unless members are versatile, the group will become frustrated and will allow even small-sized snafus to upset them completely. Since the steering committee members are trying to pass on their participative management style, one in which power is equally shared, it behooves them to seek those who are able to pick up and go on, even in the face of near-disasters.

Lastly, there is creativity. Creativity is important because Friends groups are forever in need of good ideas. Bad ideas are in surfeit; it's the good ones that are so hard to come by. Finding workers who will contribute good ideas takes time and energy, as well as a certain amount of genius. Attempting to find them from the beginning will help streamline the process more than a little.

All too often, Friends steering committees, because they are hard-pressed, or because they do not think planning the little things is important, will bring together a few friends and set about to set the Friends world aflame with "culture" (to be said as nasally as possible). What happens instead is a comedy of errors in which friends suddenly become enemies and a few individuals are stuck doing all the work. This occurs when people are selected because of their personalities, or because a few committee members know them, not because they possess one or more of the qualities mentioned above. Pick people who have proven themselves in the same or a similar capacity. But be careful not to overlook anyone. Although rare, even those who have always "wanted to do something like helping a library" may prove to be exceptional workers.

## TRAIN THE TEAM TO WORK AS A GROUP

The only knowledge the executive board members have of how a group works will be what they have learned at work or while serving with other civic groups. Or, in a worst-case scenario, they will have no knowledge at all. Take time to do the following:

- Choose members who share the same values.
- Choose members who can work together.

# POWER BROKERS

In chapter 2, brief mention was made of community power brokers. It is easy to overlook power brokers when you are putting together a Friends organization. But to do so may well spell the end of the organization before it really gets going. *Power brokers are powerful regardless of the size of the community.* In a small town, power brokers may wield power so absolutely that virtually nothing can be accomplished without their consent, explicitly or implicitly. Even more strange, this power may be used in ways that are completely invisible, or very nearly so, to the casual observer.

The steering committee may select executive board members who evince all of the traits listed above, yet the group may still fail. Why? Because no effort was made to include power brokers, even if only in consultation. If the steering committee is unable to get one or two power brokers to serve on the executive board, do not despair. The fact that someone has made an effort to consult them may be enough.

## DISCOVERING WHO THE POWER BROKERS ARE[1]

How does one go about discovering who the power brokers are in a community? A number of ways are available to the Friends organizing committee members. Three questions need to be answered:

1. Who are the members of the power structure in the community?
2. How do they go about making decisions?
3. Why do they make these decisions?

These questions will aid in understanding all the levels of decision making that go on in a community.

## THREE LEVELS OF POWER BROKERS[2]

Essentially three levels of power brokers exist. Policy makers at the top are usually made up of those industries and heads of industries that provide the town with tax support. In many cases, these are the largest industries in the town, *but not always*.

The second level of decision makers are those who are heads of banks and other smaller businesses. This also includes owners of newspapers and radio and television stations.

The third level of policy makers and decision influencers is the civic groups. Perhaps it is now more clear why these groups have been cited so often in this book. They are the first and generally the easiest of power wielders to get to know, and to get to cooperate. Because they are in the same kind of work the Friends organizer is in (nonprofit), they are usually ready to discuss mutual concerns.

# KINDS OF POWER STRUCTURES

Knowing where power brokers are likely to be merely identifies their addresses without identifying them. Knowing this alone is helpful, but it is not enough. Knowing that many mushrooms are edible is helpful, but it is far more healthy to know *which* mushrooms one can eat. Power broker identification isn't as easy as calling on the head of a major corporation or talking to a few bank presidents. The matter is much more complex than that. It is important to come to understand what *kind* of power structure one is dealing with. The kinds that Floyd Hunter identifies in *Community Power Structure* are: monopolistic, multigroup, competitive elite, and pluralistic.

## MONOPOLISTIC POWER STRUCTURES[3]

There are three main types of monopolistic community power structures: economic, political, and generational (based on family wealth).

The economic monopolistic structure manifests itself in the form of one man or one industry. But it doesn't have to be a single company in a small town; it can also be several companies that have combined their efforts to control the economic structure of the city.

The Daley machine in Chicago is a familiar example of the political monopolistic structure. The Long machine in Louisiana is another. Political monopolistic structures can work together with other members for good, or they can produce a situation in which everything has to be routed through the structure before it can be approved.

Dominance by two or more organizations or families defines the third type of monopolistic power structure. These organizations work together to make certain that some things take place and others do not. They also can take offense easily if things are done without pulling all the right levers or checking with all the right people.

## MULTIGROUP POWER STRUCTURES

Multigroup or multifamily community power structures have certain characteristics. Multigroup structures are noncompetitive. First, there are two or more power groups, each one having carved out for itself a certain niche or space in which to operate. No one group dominates entirely in such structures. But two or more groups may combine their efforts to make sure that certain initiatives succeed or fail depending on how they feel about them. Policy matters for the community usually are decided by consensus and compromise between two groups, or among three or more. Finally, there is a cohesiveness among the groups in that each one generally knows what the others are doing and why they are doing it.

## COMPETITIVE ELITE POWER STRUCTURES

The third basic power structure is the competitive elite. On the face of it, the competitive elite community power structure looks somewhat like the multigroup, but with one very important difference. There are several power groups in existence. All of them have a niche, but each or them (or most of them) are in some sort of regime conflict, either internally or with one or more of the other groups. The telltale sign of this power structure is that there is very low citizen participation in decision making. Generally, the community will allow these parties to fight matters out among themselves and let the chips fall where they may. Such a community structure is not a pleasant state of affairs. Pulling together all the warring factions is exceedingly difficult. Luckily, this power structure is not widespread.

## PLURALISTIC POWER STRUCTURES[4]

Finally, there is the pluralistic community structure. This kind of structure has a number of levels of power groups emerging as overall winners at different times and on different issues. As might be expected, this form of power structure allows for a high level of citizen participation, allowing for many different voices to be heard. Groups sharing the power in the community come to the fore when a certain issue strikes them as one upon which they wish to exert influence. Otherwise, many of the groups are generally silent, moving political pawns behind the scenes.

# POWER BROKERS AND COMMUNITY VALUES

The Friends organizer has to be aware that brokers' power can come from many different qualities: wealth, charisma, knowledge, official position, control of jobs, family ties, credit control, leadership ability, access to the media. It's easy to see from this list not only that there are many ways that power can be wielded, but that there is at least *one* for which libraries are noted: knowledge. All too often librarians knock themselves out of the running for power because they are unaware of the power they already possess. It is not necessary to rely on wealth or family name to achieve power. By using knowledge appropriately and fairly, the librarian can gain a status for the library that it has not known before.

# THREE METHODS FOR IDENTIFYING POWER BROKERS

At least three methods exist for identifying power brokers[5]: positional, reputational, and decision-making.[6] The positional method is the easiest to undertake, but the least accurate. In this method, a list is made of the individuals who hold positions of power. These positions of power are determined either by actual power possessed or by the power of the position occupied (as defined by wealth, status, occupation, or residence). Such a list would include doctors, lawyers, the mayor, and other professionals and government officials.

Once this list has been determined, one must become acquainted with as many of these individuals as possible. This method is useful as far as it goes, but the weaknesses are readily apparent. Every community has one or two individuals who have an inordinate amount of status, but who do not, by choice, occupy a position of esteem in the community. Such persons would be overlooked by the positional method.

Another approach is the reputational method.[7] This is done in exactly the same manner as the positional method at first. Then, you should talk with each of the power brokers on your list and ask them, among other things, to name the most prominent leaders in the community. Record the names of these people and ask *them* to identify who they believe are the most influential power leaders.

Eventually, this process will turn up the same names. Once this happens, you can be pretty certain that these individuals are the most prominent and most influential in the community. These are the individuals with whom you will want to become better acquainted.

The last method is known as the decision making method and it follows the same pattern as the other two. The only difference is that you ask people to identify five major decision-making *events* in the community's history, along with the names of those who made the decisions. These persons are interviewed and asked the same question, and so on, until a level of saturation or repetition occurs. This method provides the Friends organizer not only with the names of key people, but with a history of the decisions and events in the community, *and* the names of persons who helped make those decisions.

# WORKING WITH POWER BROKERS

Once you have a good idea of the kind of power structure you are dealing with, it is important to know how to work in that context. Monopolistic groups prove to be the hardest to work with, besides being the most difficult to break into. Monopolistic groups are, by definition, exclusive.

When dealing with competitive elites, you must be ready to use a number of tactics. These are warring factions who are seeking power on a number of different fronts. Various tactics you might need to try include staying above the conflict, mediating the conflict, diffusing it, attempting to integrate various viewpoints, and trying to strike compromises. In all cases, however, you should try to keep the Friends group out of the conflict, whatever it is.

# SELECTING THE FRIENDS LEADER

After you have identified power brokers and talked with civic and church group leaders, compare your list of potential leaders with the one recommended by the steering committee. Recruiting a leader is perhaps *the* most important decision in the process, since it will be to this person that the reins of the group are finally given. Finding a strong, capable person to assume this role is essential to the survival of the group.

In libraries situated in small communities, finding that one leader may seem to be next to impossible. It only stands to reason that small communities will have already identified the few capable leaders and assigned them to other tasks. But it is important to try as hard as possible, going through the list of leaders discovered through the power broker methods, and through the valuable advice of civic and church group leaders.

Should you reach the conclusion that such a leader is absent from the community, you should continue to function as the leader until one can be found. But as was pointed out previously, failure to identify that leader will endanger the Friends group in later years. Many an excellent Friends group organized by the library director or another librarian with only marginal leadership dissolved altogether, or very nearly so, when that person took another job.

The methods described above will provide the fledgling group with many names of power brokers as well as potential lay leaders. Work through the list and identify the best person for the job of Friends leader. Once this person has agreed to be the leader, the librarian's involvement will be reduced considerably.

## REMEMBER: INERTIA KILLS

Whether you are putting together ideas with staff about the first steps toward initiating a Friends group or working with a Friends steering committee, one thing is clear: lack of initiative kills. Don't let high levels of enthusiasm have a chance to cool before taking the next step. The work of identifying power brokers, for example, can go on while other preliminary steps, such as talking with members of the academic community or identifying civic organizations, continues. Don't let the organization slip away while equally important but less glamorous tasks for the Friends group are being done.

Too many would-be Friends organizers think that Friends groups will form on their own. They will not. People need to be coaxed and cajoled into action. Finding the right combination of hard-working individuals for the Friends group is perhaps the hardest task of all.

# THINGS TO DO

1. Write out an agenda of events that must come together before the Friends group can materialize. Beside each item, write down what must be accomplished in order for that objective to be achieved. Be sure to include resources needed beside each agenda item.

2. Write down the names of potential board members. Put what is known about them beside each name and write a short statement describing why that person would be a good board member. Compare your list of names with those submitted by others. Are there points of intersection? If not, why have the names been chosen?

3. Talk with others about potential board members. Look for points of agreement.

4. As time allows, talk with the members chosen for the board. In asking them to serve on the board, be sure to tell them why they were chosen.

5. Send out letters of invitation to potential board members. Send the letters out to twice as many names as needed. If they agree to serve, have them tell why they think they'll be able to help.

6. Schedule an organizational Friends meeting with all those now involved to discuss work up to this point. Hold this meeting in the library to which the Friends group is to be attached.

7. Arrange for a Friends display in the library foyer or near the circulation desk.

8. Send out letters of notice at least *two weeks* prior to the date of the meeting.

9. Announce the meeting by sending a press release to the local newspaper. The release should include the time and place of the meeting and describe the library and the Friends display.

10. *Call* each member one or two days before the meeting.

11. Hold the meeting, make assignments, give deadlines.

12. After the meeting, assess the potential of each person who attended. Schedule another meeting in less than a month, if possible.

13. Read the pertinent passages of Floyd Hunter's *Community Power Structure* and Robert Dahl's *Who Governs? Democracy and Power in an American City* (see endnotes) in order to become more familiar with the techniques described above.

14. Employ one of the methods suggested for identifying power brokers.

15. Compile a list of potential Friends leaders. Talk with each of them.

16. Present the names to the Friends steering committee and come to a consensus on who should be asked. Be sure to make the offer sound as honorific as possible, as it most certainly is.

# ENDNOTES

1. For a more thorough explanation of this process, see the following sources: Floyd Hunter, *Community Power Structure*; Robert Dahl, *Who Governs?* and *Modern Political Analysis*; Michael Aiken and Paul Mott (eds.), *The Structure of Community Power*.

2. These are not the only ways of identifying power brokers, but they are the most common. For further information, consult: Gabriel Mugny, *The Power of Minorities* (minority power structures); Alvin Toffler, *Powershift* (power structures resulting from information control); Harold Lasswell, *The Signature of Power* (a sophisticated approach to power structures); Ian Shapiro and Grant Reeher (eds.), *Power, Inequality, and Democratic Politics* (provides a good overview).

3. See Ralph Kimbrough, *Political Power and Educational Decision-Making*.

4. See Dahl, *Who Governs?* (includes an extensive investigation of this structure).

5. See Aiken & Mott, *The Structure of Community Power*, pp. 216-265.

6. See William A. Welsh, *Leaders and Elites*, pp. 183-184. Provides a compelling case in favor of using more than one approach.

7. See Hunter, *Community Power Structure*, pp. 262ff.

# 4 TOOLS FOR TEAMWORK

Once you have asked executive board members to serve, consulted power brokers, and selected the all-important Friends leader, the next step is to put together your first "official" organizing meeting.

## THE ORGANIZING MEETING

The purpose of your first public meeting is to attract additional members and supporters for your Friends group. This is your opportunity to present the goals, structure, and plans for activities developed by the steering committee to a larger audience and enlist their support in carrying those plans forward.

This kickoff meeting need not be elaborate, but it must be carefully planned to present your fledgling Friends group in the best light. If at all possible, you should hold the meeting in the library and include a tea or a reception with refreshments before or after the meeting to give the group a chance to talk informally.

The meeting should be scheduled at a time when there are few conflicting events that might draw away your audience, so you should be sure to check the academic community calendar or the schedule of events kept by an organization like the chamber of commerce. In an academic library, your should also consult your president's calendar to be sure that he or she will able to attend the event. In a public library, talk with the library director and the president of the library's board of trustees to arrange a time when they and as many trustees as possible can attend the meeting. A kickoff meeting that is missing the university president (or similarly high ranking official) or most of the library's trustees will send the message that this is an unimportant event scheduled by library zealots that can be ignored by everyone else.

You also will want to invite members of the city council and others who have responsibility for the library's support by virtue of election, appointment, politics, or employment. Consult the lists of community leaders, representatives of civic groups, power brokers, and other key library users and supporters that you and the steering committee compiled in your early organizing efforts. In an academic setting, you should consider inviting college and university administrators, faculty, and representatives of student groups. This is an opportunity to get all those with an interest in your library behind the Friends group early on.

## THINK THROUGH EVERYTHING

Putting together a kickoff event is no easy matter. It requires thinking through every facet of the event from publicity and invitations to refreshments and follow-up activities. The Friends leader and the steering committee or a special subcommittee set up to oversee the organizing meeting should take the time to draw up a careful list of all the tasks that will need to be completed to make the event successful and assign responsibilities and deadlines for carrying out those tasks to specific individuals.

Compiling this task list or work plan with the group will help to ensure that key items are not overlooked. Through the process of association (sending invitations requires stamps, having speakers may require a podium or microphones, etc.), you will be able to identify the supplies you will need to purchase or borrow and compile a budget for your event.

The steering committee will want to think through the agenda for the meeting very carefully. Remember that the primary purpose of the meeting is to explain to the audience what your Friends group is all about and enlist their support for the effort. Will the Friends leader emcee the event or is there someone else who would be more appropriate for this role? When will the library board president or the president of the college or university speak and who will deliver the introductions?

This may also be a time to present the organization's proposed constitution and bylaws and to carry out the official election of officers for your Friends group. If so, your steering committee or a special nominating committee should be prepared to explain the responsibilities of each position and to present a slate of officers for the group's consideration. You should also be prepared to handle nominations from the floor and discuss procedures for handling the actual election. For further details about the election of officers, see *Robert's Rules of Order*, Henry Davidson's *Handbook of Parliamentary Procedure*, or any other similar book. Chapter 6 outlines the functions of each committee.

# CONSTITUTION AND BY-LAWS

If you wish to incorporate your Friends group as a tax-exempt nonprofit corporation, you will need to develop a constitution or by-laws before the group can be come a legal entity. Incorporation of a Friends group is not required, but it can provide some advantages for fundraising purposes as well as stability if the group ends up with a large membership or if the makeup of the group is likely to change substantially over time. It is advisable to consult with the library's or the institution's attorneys about the advantages and responsibilities of incorporation as a nonprofit organization, as well as the specific requirements for obtaining tax-exempt status.[1]

Even if you do not choose to incorporate your group formally, it is still important to develop a constitution and by-laws to address such issues as membership fees, voting procedures and rules for establishing a quorum, the officers and committee structure of the organization, and other key operational procedures.

What does this document look like? The Friends of the Library Constitution and By-laws (usually considered a two-part document) can be as long or as short as you want it to be. The constitution does exactly that: it describes in what manner the Friends group is constituted. The by-laws portion of this organizing document outlines the operational procedures of the group.

The constitution may have at least nine parts or articles. Typically, article one states the name of the organization. Article two states the purpose of the organization. This can be spelled out in high-flown lawyer language or even higher-flown academic language. It is probably enough to say that the organization supports the interests and expansion of the library, allows for participation by members in library-related matters, and solicits gifts of all types. Examination of section 501(c)(3) of the Internal Revenue Code should be made to make certain the document is in accordance with the purposes spelled out there for tax exemption.

Article three outlines contributions (how much and how often) and whether or not these contributions are tax deductible. This is also a good place to spell out whether or not in-kind contributions are the sole ownership of the library, to be used as it sees fit. If a line such as this is omitted, the Friends groups may be setting the library up to keep in perpetuity all 500,000 words of Aunt Mabel's memoirs.

Article four outlines officers, the attendant duties to the offices, and their terms of office. A president, president-elect or vice-president, secretary, and treasurer seem to be enough for most groups.

Article five indicates how often the group will meet and what system of rules (e.g., *Robert's Rules of Order*) will govern these meetings.

Article six states how amendments will be made and whether two-thirds, one-half, a quorum, or a simple majority is needed in order to change the constitution and/or the by-laws. It is wise to indicate what constitutes a quorum here, too. Be sure to be realistic about what a quorum is. In the beginning, when the membership is, say, 30, the temptation to write in the by-laws that a quorum is a two-thirds majority is overwhelming. But when the group swells to 300, gaining a two-thirds majority may prove impossible. Many Friends groups couch all of this in legal-type language to make it look official.[2]

Article seven may refer to the by-laws of the constitution as the official procedural guide. Article eight may state something about membership and who can join. Article nine may indicate how funds will be disbursed by the Friends group.

The by-laws portion of the document may contain five or more articles with subsections. For example, the first article might spell out the classes of membership and their accompanying fees. Subsections might spell out when these fees are due, the duration of membership, and so forth (see below). Article two of the by-laws might indicate the frequency of meetings, while article three indicates the nomination and election procedures for the officers mentioned in the constitution.

Article four would then give the particulars of the committees, how they are constituted, and a list of the standing committees. Obviously these are only guidelines. The important thing is to have *something* in writing for future Friends members.

# MEMBERSHIP FEES

Membership fees are always a problem. Each group must struggle with its own identity here. Points to remember are that if the group charges a high membership fee, then the Friends group has to offer something important in return. If the "main" event is to be free to members, then the membership fee must be high enough to cover expenses. Many groups have found it best to have some nominal fee (say $15 or $25) and then offer *discounts* for all Friends activities to members. This prevents the hassle of drumming up more support to help offset the group's expenses. Obviously, the membership fees cover only the most basic of expenses. Programs should cover the bulk of what the Friends group hopes to achieve in the area of fundraising.

# TEAM BUILDING

Once the kickoff event is over, the Friends leader should meet with the executive board and newly elected or approved officers as soon as possible. The Friends leader may wish to plunge in and begin working with the group if he or she understands group dynamics fully. If not, some advice on team building may be in order.

Team building means building a group of people who are loyal to the Friends group, *almost* to a fault. Of course a group of yes-men and women who will endorse *anything* the leader wants is ill-advised. That would result in groupthink, discussed later in this chapter. What you should aim for is a group of men and women who will *work* for the library and the Friends group.

The remainder of this chapter focuses on what the Friends leader will need in order to ensure that team building is consistent and sustained. Principles outlined below will save the Friends leader much grief and struggle in the weeks and years to come.

## COMMUNICATING AND MORE

It is the job of the Friends leader to express goals in a way that everyone can understand, to *communicate* the vision. The parameters of this vision have been determined by the Friends steering committee. Some members who also served on the steering committee will bring the necessary continuity to the executive board. But the additions to the board will need to be apprised of how to work together to carry that vision out.

# FIVE STEPS TOWARD PROBLEM-SOLVING

Participative decision making (PDM) stresses five basic steps to problem-solving: the identification of problems, the collection of data, the identification of possible solutions and selection of the best alternative, the implementation of those alternatives, and evaluation.[3] PDM draws most freely on the democratic process, but is also eclectic in nature, drawing on human growth and development as well as productivity and efficiency. But how do these steps work in a "real" situation?

## IDENTIFICATION OF THE PROBLEM

Perhaps no other area is as crucial as this one. The group must come to agreement over what the problem is that is facing it. Often the leader can help in this process by pointing out a problem—lack of funding, for example—and then allowing the group to prescribe solutions. Unfortunately, problems are seldom as easily agreed upon as this. It is important that the group work together on determining what the problem is, rather than trying to solve a problem defined by someone else.

## COLLECTION OF DATA

Once a problem has been defined, as much information as possible should be gathered about previous efforts to solve it. Too often, leaders consider the problem "obvious" and then pursue what they determine to be the most "logical" solution. This can lead to befuddlement and, in some cases, outright sabotage by group members.

Data must be gathered about a problem before the group can develop an effective solution. The leader may take on this task, but it is better to involve others in the process. If the problem is a lack of funding, for example, the group will need data about past fundraising efforts, fundraising that worked and did not work, and who did the fundraising. The group also needs some perspective on the socioeconomic conditions of the region. "Solving" a funding problem by hosting a $100 a plate dinner when most of the target audience makes less than $18,000 a year is no solution.

## IDENTIFICATION OF POSSIBLE SOLUTIONS AND THE BEST ALTERNATIVE

Once the problem has been identified and agreed upon, possible solutions will come forward quickly. This part of the decision making process may take place in what is called a "blue-sky" or "brainstorming" session. Really no conceivable, logical, or legal solution to a proposed problem should be rejected. All of them should be dutifully recorded and examined by the group.

This process accomplishes two things. First, it allows everyone to participate in the solution of the problem. Second, it identifies a number of solutions, some of which the group will actually agree to implement.

During the discussion, the group will examine how the proposed solution would be carried out, how valuable it is to solving the problem, and whether or not the group can actually carry it out. By the process of elimination, refinement, and emendation, several good solutions will emerge. The Friends leader should highlight these and lead the group in a discussion of which one(s) should be implemented.

## IMPLEMENTATION

Remember the two most important words in planning: assignment and deadline. When the decision to implement a solution is made, people need to understand what they are to do and when they are to do it. If only half of this is done—if an assignment is made with no deadline—then chances are it will never be carried out, or it will always be in the process of being carried out. Any of the steps in this process may become obstacles to success. Remember to "close the sell." Making assignments and giving deadlines helps the group to achieve this.

## EVALUATION

Few groups do this part particularly well. If we broaden the analogy of a "sell" and think of this step as counting the money, it is likely that it will not be overlooked. Evaluating what happens, especially in the case of failure, prevents the same mistakes from occurring as frequently and helps to iron out places where the process failed. In all decision making, whether by group or by decree, a certain amount of failure is inevitable. By examining what happened, the leader can help the group overcome such barriers and achieve greater success the next time around.

## EQUALITY OF PARTICIPATION

The idea behind PDM is participation, and it is important to make sure that some equality of participation is going on in the group. If all members participate in shaping decisions somewhat equally, then the likelihood of the group's decisions being accepted will greatly increase, and barriers will be minimized.[4] The group is looking for an outcome, some action, and this must always be kept in mind. Groups have a natural tendency to lethargy or apathy. And why not? Each individual has these same tendencies. Bring them together in a group of six or 12 and you have magnified the problem, not diminished it. But as long as the group knows that action is expected, they will move in that direction.

# BARRIERS TO EFFECTIVE GROUPS

Groupthink[5] was singled out earlier as one of the most serious failures of groups. The symptoms are clear. Groups often get what may be called the "big head." They think they are invulnerable and that any decision they make, whether all information is present or not, will be a good one.

Groups can also fall into a rationalization process, in which members try to discredit or explain away any warnings that may be necessary for the group to know. Groups may also think that by virtue of producing a group decision, the morality of a decision is above reproach. As a result, some ethical matters may be overlooked.

Groups may fall into an "us against them" mode of thinking in which everyone outside the group is a "them." This prevents the group from getting any useful information from individuals or other groups that may be necessary for the problem's solution. Groups may also settle into procrustean conformity. At times, more vocal group members will force others into their mode of thinking or will rout out any rivals to their own version of what the decision ought to be.

Three other failings of groups include censorship, imagined unanimity, and gatekeepers. Censorship may arise in the form of members who will withhold their ideas from the group, especially if these ideas are critical of others' ideas or are against the current stream. Imaginary unanimity comes into play when the leader allows for consensual agreement to occur even though all members have not been heard, or when disagreements are not resolved, only glossed over. Silence here is often considered consent, giving the appearance of unanimity when in fact the group or the leader has failed to solicit advice or ideas from as many members as are willing to offer them. Lastly, gatekeepers are those group members who guard the group from information they think is harmful, especially information that might make the group decide differently or change from a current way of thinking.

Other less debilitating but no less destabilizing problems of groups can be found in the appropriate professional literature. The ones mentioned here are the most serious and the most common. If the leader works with the executive board carefully, as it matures, many of the problems mentioned can be avoided.

The important thing to remember is that group decision making, while difficult, is essential. Only a sustained effort to make certain that teamwork is always pursued as carefully as possible will assure a Friends group of continued success.

# OPERATIONAL PROCEDURES

Two procedural areas need to be discussed: publicity and programming. Although handled by subcommittees, the Friends leader needs to be certain this work is assigned and carried out properly. Though the publicity and programming committees will begin working later, some thought about what is needed for them to succeed will aid the selection process later.

## PUBLICITY

The publicity committee will have the responsibility for publicizing the Friends group and its activities through print and nonprint media, including newspapers, radio, and television. Given that there are at least three outlets, it might be a good idea to staff this committee with at least three members. Chapter 9 relates some of the more interesting experiences that can be had in this regard.

The work requires someone who will pound the pavement and who will make of themselves a *pleasant nuisance*. This person must always be pleasant, but also unwilling to take no for an answer. As future board members are added, their potential usefulness in helping with publicity should be considered.

The Friends leader should bring to the first board meeting the names, addresses, phone numbers, *and* contacts of every publicity facility in the area in which the Friends group will be working. Press contact should be cultivated as early as possible. The leader should find out if committee members know any of the press contacts personally and discuss strategies for establishing contact with others. Committee members should be canvassed for other media outlets that were not identified by the original community survey. If the library or the university employs a staff member with press and/or public relations responsibility, invite that person to participate as a committee member or to attend meetings as an advisor to ensure that the Friends group's message supports the ongoing work of the library and does not conflict with the university's overall mission.

The publicity committee is also responsible for sharing information about the Friends organization and its activities among the membership and to key members of the broader community. Generally, the most effective and efficient way to communicate news is through a newsletter, even if it is only a single-page document. Examples of newsletters from civic groups in the area will help the group decide what kind of newsletter it wants to produce. Examples of Friends newsletters can be obtained from FOLUSA. A newsletter will keep the membership informed, will "talk to" members when they are not together, and be a cheery substitute for a regular meeting. Such a tool is all the more important if the group is not meeting very often, or if it comes together only once or twice a year. The newsletter can be used to announce upcoming events sponsored by the Friends group and to report on them after the fact.

Publishing a newsletter is hard work, as anyone who has undertaken one knows, but it is also very gratifying. The possibilities are endless: invite the mayor to write, ask prominent citizens to remember their childhood reading experiences, allow space for local eccentrics to publish their "great" works. The newsletter is one of the best, and really one of the only, ways of keeping the group's name before its public regularly. For a few cents extra, your newsletter can be sent to thousands of people outside the membership and serve as a recruiting device as well as the group's main means of communication.

Use imagination with the newsletter, and, above all, produce one that all members can be proud of. Make sure problems of spelling, grammar, and layout are avoided. If necessary, delay production of a newsletter until you can find someone to produce a good one. Nothing works so well as a good newsletter; nothing can hurt so much as a bad one. Bear in mind that this covers only printed newsletters. If you have the capability, you might also consider transmitting electronic mail messages, limited though the potential audience may be.

These things should be kept in mind when a person is suggested to undertake the publication of the Friends newsletter. The library staff may want to publish the newsletter, or a subcommittee may be appointed to oversee it. Whether the Friends newsletter is one page or ten, it will continue to be a chief record of the group's successes, history, and evolvement for years to come.

## PROGRAMMING

This committee is responsible for advising the Board about what types of events to host, as well as actually carrying out the arrangements for events, usually with the help of subcommittees. Before this group begins its work, you should give some thought to what kind of fundraising works in the area, based on the experience of others. This group will want to be certain that its plans are not identical with those of other groups.

The Friends leader needs to come to the first meeting with a list of ideas about what kinds of fundraising programs work best in the area based on the community study conducted earlier. Of course, the committee will bring its own knowledge of community events to the table, but it also helps to have *some* direction from the executive committee and the Friends leader.

The frequency of program events may have been outlined in the by-laws, or it could be left to the discretion of the executive committee or even the program committee. A Friends group can have as many programs as it feels energetic enough to host. But ardor should be tempered by the realization that any event, for 50 or for 500, is very hard work. One way to handle this would be to have at least one really spectacular event (a citywide auction, a speaker's dinner) that will draw a lot of press attention on its own merits and a few smaller programs (a poetry reading, a library exhibit) to occur at different times during the year. This will take some brainstorming from the members of the executive board. But the program committee, after kicking around a few ideas, should be able to come up with at least one event that will fulfill all of the following criteria:

1. Appropriateness to the stated purpose of the Friends group.
2. Ability to attract attention on its own merits. (Your event should get the attention of the press even if you don't invite them.)
3. Level of interest that justifies charging community participants.
4. Cost-effectiveness. (Your event should be economical to put on and profitable to pull off.)

# THINGS TO DO

1. Read Conway's article "The Myth, Mystery, and Mastery of Participative Decision Making in Education" in *Education Administrative Quarterly* 20 (1984), pages 11-40, and Zander's book *Making Groups Effective* (see bibliography). Conway has written what amounts to an expose of participative decision making, and Zander has written a hymn in its honor.

2. Talk to someone who has worked with groups and has instituted participative decision making, either in a Friends group or library setting.

3. Make a test run with the executive board. Ask them to decide a matter by giving them an assignment and a deadline. The test could be some decision that really needs to be made, but isn't all that crucial. Follow the steps of identifying the problem, providing the proper data, listing the solutions, implementing them, and then reviewing the results.

# ENDNOTES

1. For more information, see David J. Webster and Joseph A. Kowar, "Tax-Exempt Status," in Sandy Dolnick (ed.), *Friends of the Library Sourcebook*, pp. 43-51.
2. See Bill Katz, *The How-To-Do-It Manual for Small Libraries*, pp. 312-313.
3. R. Campbell and W. Wayson, "Decision Making in the Elementary Principalship," *National Elementary Principal* 41: 17-22. See also A. Zander, *Making Groups Effective*.
4. J. Bartunek and C. Kepys, "Participation in School Decision Making," *Urban Education* 14: 52-75. See also K. Lewin, "Frontiers in Group Dynamics I," *Human Relations* 1: 1-39.
5. See I.L. Janis, *Victims of Groupthink* and Janis, *Groupthink: Psychological Studies of Policy Decisions and Fiascoes*.

# 5 PROGRAMS FOR FRIENDS GROUPS

Chapter 1 included several examples of fundraising programs planned by library Friends groups. In this chapter, several other kinds of programs are examined along with how you go about developing them for presentation to a Friends group.[1]

## FRIENDS GROUP ACTIVITIES

In Chapter 1, I mentioned the importance of "rallying" a Friends group. One way of "rallying" is to decide on an activity and then examine its structural needs. The subsequent chapters of this book are devoted to exploring how the Friends leader marshals forces together to put on a major annual event. Although the focus is primarily on an annual dinner event, the ideas may be easily adapted for any of the activities listed below.

### BOOK SALES

These may be held every week, once a month, or a few times each year. Depending on the return desired, book sales can be very elaborate, or they can be run in "spare time." There are book companies that will come in, set up your sale, and display the books. They will also want about 30 to 50 percent of the "take." It may be more profitable to sell obsolete books from the library's collection or books from patrons' attics. Books from patrons' attics, however, will present the problem of disposing of books that do not sell. Make certain that each patron who donates books knows they will not be returned.

To have a successful book sale, you need about six weeks for planning and implementation. This does *not* include the time needed to collect the books, which should be ongoing throughout the year. The schedule might include the following:

**Week One:** Decide on whether to oversee the sale yourself or have an outside company undertake it.

**Weeks Two and Three:** If the Friends group handles it, turn over the logistics to the program committee and have members gather items, price them, and solicit workers for the actual sale.

**Weeks Four and Five:** Advertise the sale (see the section in chapter 4 on publicity).

**Week Six:** Prepare for the onslaught with tables, displays, and about $50 in cash to make change (stock with plenty of ones and lots of coin change).

Putting on a book sale requires collecting books months in advance of the event. The library at the State University of New York (SUNY), Albany, sponsors an annual book sale. The books are collected all year long and then placed on tables on a well-publicized date. Unsold volumes are either held until next year or sold to book dealers after the sale.

The Friends of the Public Library of Bristol, Virginia (population 25,000), puts on an annual book sale consisting of donated books and those retired from the library's collection. The sale nets several hundred dollars each year.

But a book sale does not need to be conventional. The Friends of the Louisiana State University Library in Baton Rouge won the 1988 Friends of Libraries USA Award in part for the huge Book Bazaar they put on each year. More than 300 volunteers work together for the event. The sale focuses on the resale of used textbooks to students. Books are collected all year long and stored in the library's Book Barn. Nearly 60,000 books are collected for the sale. The leftovers are sold to book dealers. The group raises nearly $40,000 from the Book Bazaar.

## MEMORABILIA SALES

This type of sale might include tee shirts with the library's logo, bookmarks and pens, tote bags, mugs, and every and any other type of item. These items could be sold in conjunction with another Friends event, placed out in the public library lobby at different times during the year, or sold at a special sale. For academic libraries, memorabilia may also be sold in college bookstores.

## RUMMAGE SALES

Rummage sales can be very useful and highly successful if they are well-planned. The event also needs to be well-publicized and should draw from as many possible sources as can be found. Be sure to reserve the right to "inspect" the merchandise. Rummage sales need about a six- to eight-week period for the collection and inspection of merchandise and about five to six weeks for planning and implementation.

Some libraries may want to combine this event with another organization, such as the Junior League, and host one huge rummage sale. When a sale is scheduled with another group, both share expenses, but both also share profits. Friends groups risk losing their identities when paired too often with other groups.

Like the book sale, collection of materials for a rummage sale must be done ahead of time, so having storage space is essential. Pricing will also need to be done. The place where all the items can be displayed without a great deal of difficulty to those interested in buying them should be handicap accessible with adequate parking. Members will be need to be recruited to work as cashiers and salespersons, depending on the size of the sale. If clothes are offered, a place offering adequate privacy for trying them on must be available.

While such sales are more typically associated with public libraries, no prohibitions are etched in stone forbidding academic libraries to host them.

## AUCTIONS

These especially successful events must be planned months in advance and need widespread publicity. Items must be rounded up from donors, and an auctioneer must usually be hired. While hugely successful in some cases, the use of auctions by public radio and television stations may diminish the number of donated items available to Friends groups. Auctions need a minimum of about three or four months for planning. The first month should be devoted to securing donated items. By the end of the first six weeks, it should be obvious whether the auction will be possible. If only a few items have been collected, the auction may need to be postponed until more "merchandise" can be found. Civic groups, businesses, religious groups, and individual patrons of the library are good places to begin searching for the merchandise to be auctioned off.

Gustavus Library Associates of Gustavus Adolphus College in St. Peter, Minnesota, raised more than $130,000 with a silent auction, which was also accompanied by a dinner and entertainment. The event won the Friends group the 1990 FOLUSA award. More than 600 items were gathered for the auction in advance. Corporate gifts also were added to the coffers.

## LUNCHEONS

While similar to dinner events, luncheons are usually shorter and do not require the presence of a well-known speaker. Such programs really must be kept to a maximum of ninety minutes, unless your target audience are people who do not work. Luncheons may focus on one of the library's collections or may showcase a local talent.

The Friends of the Library at SUNY, Albany, host a regular luncheon once known as "Wednesday Wanderings" (it was later renamed "Community Conversations"). This is a noontime lecture-luncheon series that features faculty research. It has attracted widespread interest.

## LECTURE SERIES

Many academic Friends groups sponsor lecture series. After all, they have right on hand a number of lecturers just itching to be showcased. Many public libraries have also had success hosting lecture series. This kind of series may focus on a special collection in the library or may rally around a theme the library wishes to stress.

The lecturers *must* be entertaining. Dr. Dryasdust may be adequate for the teaching profession, but he or she simply will not do for the Friends event. If Dr. Dryasdust does give a lecture, future lectures will be well-publicized—adversely—in the community. It is therefore a good idea to hear the lecturer before the audience does. This may not be necessary if the lecturer is a highly successful speaker on the lecture circuit.

Augustana Library Associates at Augustana College, Sioux Falls, South Dakota, won the 1987 FOLUSA award for, among other things, its lecture series. The event focused on "Shaw and Friends: An Irish Festival," and showcased the library's magnificent 400-volume collection of works by and about the famed Irish-born playwright George Bernard Shaw. The lecture series made up only one part of an extensive program that also included play performances, a photography exhibit, and a night of Irish music.

## ANTIQUE SHOWS

Some libraries may opt for the unconventional and host an antique show. The antique show is very much like the auction, the only difference being that antiques are collected and then sold. Such an undertaking requires at least eight months to plan and execute. Collection of antiques should take place six months to a year prior to the planning and implementation stages. Again, seeing the antiques ahead of time will save time and prevent a lot of unnecessary chagrin. This should be enough warning that Friends groups should avoid making a general call for "any items" when putting on a sale, whether it be books, antiques, or clothes. Such a general call will result in a general mess at your sale. Of course, the old saw that beggars cannot be choosers is in effect here, but it need not be taken to extremes.

The Friends of the Lovejoy Library at Southern Illinois University in Edwardsville have had spectacular success with antique shows. (The group also has a 1991 FOLUSA award to show for its efforts.) Although not the only Friends event (they also have a book fair and used textbook sale), the annual antique show is one of the group's brighter highlights. Attended by more than 1,900 people, the antique show has not only attracted much publicity, but also much needed funding.

## MISCELLANEOUS ACTIVITIES

Some Friends activities defy categorization. A champagne gala is one unconventional but nonetheless successful event (as practiced by the Friends of the Library at Tennessee Tech University). The champagne gala allows Friends members to congregate for fun, festivities, and, of course, funds. The Friends of the New York Public Library hosts several parties in private homes during the year to raise funds for the library. The Friends of the Library of the University of Illinois at Urbana-Champaign conduct a telethon to raise funds. The Friends group also sponsors a major benefit each year, raising nearly $10,000.

The Friends of the Library of Augustana College also sponsors "A Winter's Tale," a program that is devoted to literature and music. While widely attended by the community, the event is *not* a fundraising event.

Vanderbilt University Friends focus on an annual speaker-dinner event. The library at King College in Bristol, Tennessee, focused on an annual dinner held in the fall of each year. Because the nature of these events requires special planning, details of speaker-dinner events will be explored in subsequent chapters.

Friends of public libraries may wish to take the topical approach. For example, a public library Friends group might consider a program on latchkey children. Another Friends group may wish to host a program on retirement.

No matter what the event, the Friends leader, in conjunction with the executive board members, should try hard to avoid any scheduling conflicts. If the event is held in the fall, a Friends event scheduled on a Friday night will interfere with Friday night high school football games. While executive board members may never attend these games, someone should point out that many parents and friends do. A check with the local chamber of commerce will help Friends groups come up with a date that will not interfere with existing programs in the community.

# WHAT IF THE EVENT IS A FLOP?

It can happen even to the best Friends events. Due to bad weather, poor timing, or any number of other setbacks, sometimes an event fails miserably. What then? Without equivocation, the event can be still be *reported* as a success. Even if only ten people showed up, something happened. Be sure to relate whatever happened at the event in the newsletter, if one is printed, and also in local press releases.

## HOW TO AVOID PITFALLS

How do you avoid disaster? Unfortunately, no fail-safe plan exists, but there are some points that may help to minimize the likelihood of failure.

- *Ask* other community and civic members what they are doing and what has and has not worked.
- *Talk* with Friends members to get some idea of what they think a library is and what it should do.
- *Find out* if they are capable of helping in some way: with work, with contributions, with ideas.

# DELEGATING THE WORK

The work of programming should fall to the program committee. That committee should examine every aspect of a Friends event, making sure that all the details are taken care of and that scheduling conflicts have been avoided. The role of the Friends leader is to oversee the work being done. The work of the library director is behind the scenes, but making sure the lay leader is doing his or her job. Successful annual events require that everyone work together.

# THINGS TO DO

1. Talk with the development office or your board of trustees about compiling a list of potential donors. If the Friends group is attached to a public or special library, look over registration cards with an eye to building a list of 100 names to augment membership rolls.

2. Suggest to the executive board several fundraising events: a tea, a reading, an Honor-Your-Library day, or some other events. Present the list to board members and ask for their suggestions.

3. Once a fundraising event has been decided on, make a list of all the things that will be needed in order for that event to be successful. Once this list is complete, separate it into one list of needed items and another list of cost items. Of course, some items may appear on both lists.

4. Prepare a budget for the event by walking through each step. Consult the executive board for missing pieces. Make assignments as needed. If funding for the items is needed before the event can be held, ask members of the board how they can help.

5. Announce the event in the print and nonprint media. If appropriate, send invitations to selected community members. Add an RSVP on the bottom of the invitation.

6. After the event, schedule a board meeting to assess what worked and what did not. Ask for advice on reporting on the event in the newsletter.

7. Be sure to send thank-you letters to all who helped.

# ENDNOTE

1. For more information about the programs mentioned in this section, see Jon Eldredge, "More Valuable Than Money," *College and Research Libraries News* 52: 635-639.

# 6 THE FIRST ANNUAL EVENT

Murphy's Law works overtime for Friends organizations and especially for their events. Organizing an event will take all the time alloted to it. If something can go wrong, it will. But don't be dismayed. Working with the human equation in other settings should provide the necessary immunization to the slings and arrows hurled during the planning and implementation of an annual event.

## ANNUAL EVENTS

First, what is meant by an annual event? This is no trick question. An annual event is *anything* the Friends of the Library hosts each year. It does not have to be a show-stopping follies performance, but it should be *a planned event that brings together most members of your Friends group, showcases some aspect of the library, attracts new Friends members, and raises much-needed support.* It may well be that, depending on the size and energy of your Friends group and the level of community interest, you will choose to hold a major event twice or even three times a year. Then again, after hosting such an event, you may find that every other year is often enough to put together a major event.

### TYPES OF ANNUAL EVENTS
Your annual event could be a dinner or a luncheon, a book or bake sale, an auction, a marathon—in short, any event that captures the imagination of members and seeks to draw crowds in large numbers. The basic steps outlined in this chapter can be applied, with necessary adaptations, to virtually any annual event chosen by a Friends group.

### DECIDING ON AN ANNUAL EVENT
The annual event should provide a forum in which discussing culture, libraries, and money will not appear incongruous. If the approach of your group is the proverbial high road, and that approach is one that will be supported by the community, then the annual event is not likely to be mud-wrestling. Within the context of what the Friends group hopes to accomplish, and within the boundaries of what the community will support, the event chosen can be virtually anything.

Friends of public libraries may be less restricted in the variety of programs they are able to host than their academic counterparts.

While this is not true regarding the political or social milieu, public libraries do not typically carry the weight of academia that colleges and universities do. Of course, no written rule states that, for example, an academic library cannot host a pie-throwing contest aimed at administrators. Chances are, such an event would be very popular among students. But pie-throwing fundraisers hosted on academic campuses must be done on a case-by-case basis. Some college or university officials simply would not allow for any program that detracted from the real or imagined intellectual tradition that has been established at the college or university.

Author-dinner events appeal to large numbers of people, give the appearance of giving a lot while costing only a little, and showcase the library and the Friends group liberally. They also blend in with the emphasis on books and ideas. Of course, no such emphasis is required. Authors write books on every subject from the arcane to the ridiculous to the sublime. Choice of the speaker will be based on the group's discussion of available speakers and the purpose of your Friends group.

## CHOOSING SPEAKERS—LOCAL OR NATIONAL?

Friends groups may choose from a cadre of local speakers, or they may choose regional speakers who bring to the Friends dais enthusiasm and support for its objectives. One might think that a local speaker would be the most logical choice, and the one most likely to gain the greatest amount of support from the community, but such is not always the case.

Local talent may not be of the highest caliber, may be overexposed, and may not have the highest audience drawing power. Of course, disasters have occurred with national speakers because expectations were raised so high that failure was inevitable, and condemnation resounding. Since, however, nationally known individuals have a reputation to protect, they tend to be successful more often in pleasing audiences than untried or inexperienced local talent. If local or regional talent is used, be sure a number of your group has seen or heard them perform.

National talent is recommended for one very important reason: audience drawing power. Nothing is more difficult than to pull modern people away from their self-imposed solitary confinement to television. If the annual event is a talking head, so to speak, then more than three-fourths of the program's success depends on the average citizen being able to recognize that talking head immediately, *by name*.

A national name (such as William F. Buckley, Jr., or Walter Cronkite) has instant name recognition, a vital ingredient for attracting an audience unless unlimited funds for publicity are available. Because most Friends organizations are trying to attract funds for *library* use, it stands to reason that efforts would be made to attract large numbers of people for a low overhead. This is impossible if the audience is forever asking, "Now who is this speaker you've got coming and why should I give up my precious free time?"

Of course not *everyone* inside and outside the library community will be attracted to the annual event. Don't even try to attract them all. Try instead to meet the goals and objectives your group has established and then work to fine tune the event according to the number of individuals it attracts.

## CHOICE WEEDS

Whatever event is chosen, it will, by that choice, weed out some members of your community. By the same token, whoever is selected as the speaker at a speaker-dinner event will also eliminate some of the potential audience. By relying on a nationally known figure, some "downsizing" of the audience that occurs naturally will be avoided.

## WHEN TO HOST AN EVENT

Deciding when the annual event will occur is entirely up to the executive board (with advice coming from the program committee). Early fall (mid-September to late October) and spring (weather permitting, mid-March through May) seem to be the best times for academic library groups. Special and public libraries can choose virtually any time. Summer, however, is an especially bad time. Not only are library staffs on vacation, but so are many people in the community. We tend to fill all the "free" time we have in the summer with activities other than Friends events.

Choosing the season should be governed, in large part, by the climate. Even highly cultivated members do not like to go out in inclement weather. While this is less true in the North than it is in the South, experience shows that individuals are less likely to venture out under poor weather conditions, if they have a choice. Rather than provide potential or would-be patrons with a suitable reason for not attending the annual event by planning it to coincide with hurricanes, tornadoes, or blizzards, why not choose another time when weather is less of a factor?

## MARGINS FOR ERROR

The first annual event allows *more* room for forgiving error than do successive ones. How can this be true? After the first event, the group has only one year to plan the next. With the first one, the group may take as much time as it needs to plan, announcing the annual event when it feels it is ready. But once an *annual* event is announced, the clock begins ticking away for the next one the moment the first one ends.

## A CHECKLIST FOR THE ANNUAL EVENT

What goes into planning such an event? Following is a checklist of things that should be taken into consideration for an annual dinner event, with attendant committees specified.

1. Speaker recruitment (program committee)
2. Setting a date (program committee)
3. Choosing a site; determining a menu (accommodations and table arrangements committees)
4. Choosing a theme (table committee)
5. Publicity (publicity committee)
6. Invitations (publicity committee)
7. Alerting the press (publicity committee)
8. Preparing for speaker's arrival (accommodations committee)
9. Researching the speaker (program committee)

It would be an easy argument to make that each item on the agenda could be handled by a subcommittee of the program committee. But do not multiply committees without necessity. The following committees appear to be essential.

**Program Committee:** The program committee is responsible for speaker recruitment and one member of the committee, preferably the chair, should be in constant contact with the speaker to act as a liaison with other committees, such as the publicity and arrangements committees. The program committee should also decide if library memorabilia will be sold at the event. A member of this committee should see that books written by the speaker are on hand for sale and autographing (if the speaker is willing). Although not required, it is highly desirable if each member of this committee serve in some capacity on one of the subcommittees listed below.

The program committee must come up with program funding ideas that will work. Committee members also need to remember that programs can be held *independently* of fundraising, though this is not always the best kind of marriage. For example, the committee could decide to have a readathon, sellathon, walkathon—whatever—in order to raise funds for the Friends. These events may be very successful, but be sure to make it clear that this is a Friends group event so that participants will not confuse it with other nonprofit fundraisers such as the March of Dimes or Crisis Pregnancy Centers.

Remember that the type of Friends group—academic or public—will have a bearing on the type of fundraising the committee can do. In some libraries, virtually anything goes: from belly dancing to gala auctions. In more austere settings, there may not be any *stated* objection to a certain kind of fundraising, but the program committee must be sensitive to the unstated taboos of academic fundraising.

It is much better to hold a carefully planned event, an auction, a speaker's dinner, or a public reading, that is tied to the need for funding. This can be done in a double-sure fashion by charging for the event and then asking for funding again during the event. Losses can be recouped by having lots of memorabilia on sale to raise even more funds.

**Publicity Committee:** This committee is responsible for getting the information out to all media outlets, setting up interviews and press conferences for the speaker, getting out press releases, making contact with all civic groups, churches, and temples, and providing information on the speaker (usually obtained from the speaker's bureau or agent). This committee is also in charge of printing invitations and getting them mailed out, and for issuing the newsletter (if one is used) in time to alert members of the coming event.

If the steering committee has done its spade work well, at least one member of this committee will be a member of the press in your town.

**Accommodations Committee:** This committee has the task of finding suitable hotel accommodations, making certain the dinner site is suitable, confirming flight arrangements, and providing transportation for the speaker to and from the airport to the event site. The head of the program committee should be a part of this effort, since he or she will be in contact with the speaker most often.

At least one member of this committee should scout out the accommodations *before* the speaker settles in them. In the case of the dinner site, wheelchair-accessible accommodations should be checked out.

**Table Arrangements:** This committee will make sure that the dinner site location *looks* attractive, that the meal is suitable, and that library paraphernalia is on hand to sell—things such as mugs, t-shirts, and other memorabilia. This committee, in concert with the accommodations committee, should determine a suitable theme that is approved by the program committee.

Staffing for each committee will have to be determined by practice. As mentioned earlier, you might need three people for the publicity committee because there are three main types of media outlets (radio, television, and newspapers). A fourth could be added to cover unconventional media outlets. Staffing of committees largely depends on the energy and enthusiasm of those appointed to them. In some cases, three will get the job done; in others, three hundred might not be enough.

# BUDGETING FOR THE EVENT

Nothing dampens enthusiasm for Friends groups more than the thought of money and where it is going to come from. Although some Friends groups fund their events entirely from receipts that come in during the weeks leading up to the event, some budget projections need to be estimated.

The worksheet in Figure 6-1 is a guide to budgeting the Friends event. While one successful Friends event may spawn a school of others, the first event may be planned more on faith than actual dollars. This is the kind of talk that makes budget officers not long for this world, and Friends groups short on longevity. But some free-wheeling budgeting *has* to be assumed, since money in hand is not always possible. If the money *must* be in hand before any work can be done, your event may be a long time in coming. Of course, the executive board must understand that it is responsible for any unpaid bills in the event of the unspeakable—failure.

The worksheet is for cost items you know you will have. After you put down estimated costs, you may have to readjust them after the speaker's fee has been negotiated, the hotel accommodations have been confirmed, and caterers have been hired. Figure 6-2 shows what the worksheet looks like when filled in for an actual event.

While the budgeted amount fell short on some events we sponsored, the difference was always made up by a larger than expected audience, special events held and individually charged for, or other

FIGURE 6-1    Budget Worksheet for Friends Event

## ESTIMATED EXPENSES

|                                                    | Budget | Actual |
|----------------------------------------------------|--------|--------|
| Publicity                                          |        |        |
|   Invitations - Printing                 | _____ | _____ |
|   Invitations - Postage                  | _____ | _____ |
|   Brochures/Posters - Printing           | _____ | _____ |
|   Newsletter - Postage                   | _____ | _____ |
|   Other                                  | _____ | _____ |
| Room Rental                                        | _____ | _____ |
| Sound System                                       | _____ | _____ |
| Table Decorations                                  | _____ | _____ |
| Speaker                                            |        |        |
|   Fee                                    | _____ | _____ |
|   Travel/Hotel/Food                      | _____ | _____ |
| Memorabilia                                        |        |        |
|   Mugs/Shirts/Pens/etc.                  | _____ | _____ |
| Other Expenses                                     | _____ | _____ |
|   SUBTOTAL                               | _____ | _____ |
| Expected No. of Attendees                          | _____ | _____ |
| Cost per person                                    | _____ | _____ |
|   (divide cost by no. of attendees)      |        |        |
| Meal cost per person                               | _____ | _____ |
| TOTAL COST PER PERSON                              | _____ | _____ |

unexpected dividends. Examples of some of those "extras" are discussed in chapter 8.

You may be wondering where the dollars for the first event come from. You can hold a book sale, sponsor some readathons, walkathons, or bake sales, but you do not have to. Generally speaking, when trustees or administrators are given a clear picture of what such a program could mean, most are happy to make the financial commitment necessary to cover the first year's costs.

# SPEAKER RECRUITMENT

Speakers should be chosen to coincide with local interests as nearly as possible. This is not as crucial as other matters on the checklist, but it always helps if the program committee can find someone who can speak on a topic that many community members are interested in. The best way to determine what topic this might be is to examine the local paper. What are the local events (as well as national) that fill its pages? Many ideas can be gleaned from local newspapers.

It's also a good idea to examine weekly and monthly popular magazines. Quite a number of people in the community are likely to subscribe to *Time, Newsweek, U.S. News and World Report,* or some other national publication. Without arguing the relative merits of any of these, suffice it to say that what appears in the pages of two or more of these magazines is likely to be of some concern to members of the Friends target community. But do not choose an event specific to a given week. By the time the event takes place, it may no longer be important.

The program committee might also choose a speaker who is known for humor or outspokenness. But avoid getting a speaker whose humor is off-color, or whose outspokenness is simply blatantly offensive.

It is important that the program committee choose a speaker whose fee can be recouped—and then some. It is, of course, pointless to invite a speaker whose fee will all but exceed the gross take. Determining this figure is entirely community-driven. If your community is largely rural with a very small weekly newspaper, hosting a Friends annual event that showcases an intellectual may not succeed—unless he or she charges practically nothing. On the other hand, a humorous columnist or a well-known comedian may reap huge dividends. Earlier research on the community, and

---

FIGURE 6-2   Sample Worksheet from Actual Event

## ESTIMATED EXPENSES

|  | Budget | Actual |
|---|---|---|
| Publicity |  |  |
| Invitations - Printing | $150 | $127.50 |
| Invitations - Postage | $50 | $35.50 |
| Brochures/Posters - Printing | $50 | $45.23 |
| Newsletter - Postage | $550 | $425.25 |
| Other | $100 | $238.60[a] |
| Room Rental | $110 | $25[b] |
| Sound System | $0 | $0[c] |
| Table Decorations | $250 | $125.60[d] |
| Speaker |  |  |
| Fee | $5,000 | $3,500 |
| Travel/Hotel/Food | $200 | $325[e] |
| Memorabilia |  |  |
| Mugs/Shirts/Pens/etc. | $550 | $490.23 |
| Other Expenses | $200 | $250 |
| SUBTOTAL | $7,210 | $5,587.91 |
| Expected No. of Attendees | 400 | 475 |
| Cost per person (divide cost by no. of attendees) | $18.02 | $11.76 |
| Meal cost per person | $6.50 | $5.75 |
| TOTAL COST PER PERSON | $24.52 | $17.51 |

NOTES:
a. Costs included pewter mugs sold specially.
b. A nominal cleaning fee was charged for a campus facility.
c. No charge was issued for the sound system.
d. Library staff members helped make many of the decorations.
e. This fee cannot be controlled as it is added by the speaker.

earlier discussion with other similar groups, should help determine what speaker would be best for the community.

## INVITING A SPEAKER

The program committee must realize, and early on, that their invitation to a popular speaker will be one of perhaps hundreds that he or she will receive *that week*. What will distinguish your letter from the others? What will make a lasting impression? One way to make your request unique is to play upon the *distinctiveness* of the group and the library. Find some angle, some aspect of who and what the library is about that will appeal to and convince the speaker to read further—and to make plans to come and speak.

Identifying distinctiveness is not enough. The program committee must also convey that distinctiveness in an agreeable manner that will grab the attention of the would-be speaker and cause him or her to say, "Now this looks interesting!" Perhaps the following example will help clarify this point.

An editor friend of mine told me about a query letter he once received from a writer. Query letters are the most common way writers get their material before an editor. The query letter has to be as good as the manuscript it introduces, maybe even better. Obviously, if the query fails to arouse curiosity, the manuscript will go unread. My friend told me he opened his mail one morning and read the following:

"Darling! How I long to be with you, how I need to see you. But how to get by *him*? He will be at work soon and then, oh then, the moments we can spend together in one another's arms!"

Imagine my friend's surprise. It was only after another paragraph in a similar vein that the writer indicated how she wanted to write an article for his religious publication on infidelity in marriage, providing a glimpse of "what happens when the panting subsides." My friend snatched up the opportunity and gave the unheralded writer a try.

Writing a letter of invitation to would-be speakers poses many of the same problems. You must grab their attention, leave a memorable impression, and describe the speaking opportunity. The following letter-writing tips might also be instructive.

## 1. Don't Be Negative

Never, never (even when true) open an invitation with a negative statement such as, "I know you don't know me or my library, but. . . ." Be firm and positive with your image. Tell what must be told, but tell it truthfully. Don't spend a lot of time trying to gain the speaker's sympathy. Begin right away with the important matter at hand.

## 2. Never Beg Off a Fee

Do not put in the letter that your group is poor, or that your institution or the library is indigent, and beg the speaker to come gratis. Do talk about the fact that you have limited resources and use the opportunity to ask for a schedule of speaking fees. But never try to beg off the fee. Later, if the *speaker* brings up the subject of reducing the fee or writing it off as a contribution, the offer may be gladly accepted. (Don't, however, hold your breath.)

## 3. Don't Stretch the Truth

Don't make promises that will be impossible to keep, and don't offer any contingencies for things that are not absolutely certain. Never tell a speaker that the fee will be covered *if* so many attend. Also, never tell a speaker that they will be meeting the mayor and the Chamber of Commerce, get the keys to the city, and spend the day being transported around town in a Rolls Royce, *unless* all of this is already set up. The temptation to put something in the letter to make the event seem more desirable than it is will be strong, but resist it and tell the simple truth as elegantly as possible.

## 4. Don't Speak the Local Vernacular

Write the letter with impeccable grammar. When it is completed, give it to someone who knows about these things, such as an English teacher or an editor—anyone who will be able to catch the gaffes that are probably there. Not all speakers care about this, of course, but many do. If the first impression of your group is a letter with grammatical errors, typos, and many corrections with liquid paper, it will not easily be forgotten. After all, even though the person doing the writing for the group may have completed ten impeccable reports, 14 error-free letters, and 17 flawless brochures that day, the letter with the mistakes is all that the speaker will see of the Friends group. If it looks unprofessional, that is the impression that will be left.

### 5. Don't Mail a Tome

Some people seem to think that if you inundate the speaker with your library's annual report, the latest yearbook (if an academic library), a quarterly publication produced by the college or the city, and the library's newsletter (not to mention pictures of the children and the grandchildren), you will surely win the heart of a potential speaker. Nothing could be further from the truth. If what you are mailing will not fit in a small standard or even a legal size envelope, then it's probably too much information. Since all the materials you send will not be kept, even if the speaker agrees to come, save the tome to send closer to the event.

### WHAT TO SEND

So, what *should* be included? Along with the letter, it is a good idea to enclose a copy of the Friends newsletter. (See why they're so handy?) You should also include one or two recent but small pictures of the library, and maybe a small pamphlet about the library, the group, or the city, if a public library. *No more* than this is necessary. The long and short of it is this: Send just enough to arouse curiosity, but never enough to satiate it. The more that is left to mystery, the more likely the speaker will be convinced he or she really must come to the event.

### WHAT TO SAY

Letters begin in many different ways, but the best for this purpose begin with a narrative about the library, the college (if an academic library), or the community (if a public library). Beginning with something other than the library may help make telling the story easier. Are there unusual circumstances surrounding the college or the town? Turn them into interesting *short* stories. Suppose the library is situated in a mountain range. Why not begin by saying, "Nestled among quilted mountains of orange, brown, and yellow is a small library that has stood the test of time. For more than a hundred years, it continues as a stalwart guardian of truth for its patrons, offering a sure intellectual footing . . ." Get the picture? For someone fighting city traffic, this image might prove irresistible.

A good letter should include at least some of the following: history, scenery, humanity, and genuineness. Focus on the history of the group, underscoring some aspect of that history that might appeal to the speaker. Include some scenery of the area, if you think this is appropriate. Show something of the humanity of the group, but don't overdo it. And finally, be genuine, not clever or inappropriately humorous.

# SPEAKER'S BUREAUS

Let's suppose that your speaker answers the invitation with, "I'll be delighted to speak at your library dinner. Someone from my speaker's bureau will be in touch with you soon." Now, what do you do? Think "negotiation" and "compromise." While most speaker's bureaus are above board and helpful, they all bring with them a number of drawbacks. The problems that occur with speaker's bureaus are not insurmountable, but neither are they insignificant.

**Note:** A speaker's bureau should not be confused with the speaker's agent. Writers, for example, often have someone from their publisher set up their speaking engagements. This is a natural alliance since it helps the publisher sell books. None of the problems discussed below refer to a speaker's agent, publisher, or book representative. Agents are discussed in more detail later.

## HOW SPEAKER'S BUREAUS CAN HINDER YOU

The first problem associated with speaker's bureaus is that they make it difficult for you to get in touch with the speaker. From the moment a bureau is engaged, third party communications begin. This means that when something comes up—a large organization wants to help underwrite the dinner, or a television station wants to do a live interview—someone must write or call the bureau who will, in turn, write or call the speaker. The speaker answers the bureau, and the bureau eventually responds to someone in the Friends group. Communications of this type cannot be handled in a matter of days, but this is often all the time you have!

Second, changes in the original agreement frequently occur. When a bureau is involved, nearly *every* change requires a request in writing. You might even be charged extra if the speaker is asked to greet the mayor or say a few words upon arrival. The bureau is under strict contractual guidelines with the speaker to book events. If the original contract calls for an after-dinner speech, and a local organization wants the speaker to say a few words on behalf of a charity, what happens then? The bureau must approve it first. The bureau's meticulous care for the speaker is understandable—they do not want to lose the speaker as a client, nor do they want to soil their good name among other potential speakers.

Then there is the problem of making arrangements. Agenda, hotel accommodations—in short, everything must be sent through a third party. The whole experience is like courting through a friend. The excitement of courtship may still be present, but none of the enjoyment is.

Speakers *can* be difficult to please, so any accommodation arrangements ought to be checked through the bureau for approval before they are finalized. Unfortunately, however, the bureau may or may not know if the accommodations are acceptable to the speaker and may have to "get back to you," leaving you dangling for two or three weeks.

Then there is the problem of charges. Dealing directly with speakers can save the group money—maybe even as much as $1,500 *per speaker*. This is especially true of lesser known speakers.

Finally, there is the fact that the speaker's bureau is in the business of getting lots of speakers lots of engagements. The bureau staff member assigned to your event will probably have two dozen or more similar engagements for other speakers going on simultaneously. If the Friends group happens to land a speaker who is less than a household name (which translates into less profit for the bureau) it may get less attention than their more profitable clients.

## HOW SPEAKER'S BUREAUS CAN HELP YOU

Does all of this mean that bureaus should be avoided? No, it doesn't. It is highly unlikely that they *can* be avoided. Sometimes there isn't any choice. And even with all the disadvantages, there still remain some advantages to working with speaker's bureaus.

First, the people in the bureaus tend to be delightful to work with. They are hard workers and are generally available day or night to help. Though they have very little control over the timing of things, they usually try to respond to inquiries when a deadline is pressing.

Second, they are a great help with publicity and will provide pointers on how the publicity package they send should be used. The *publicity package* itself is very helpful. Working without a bureau means getting one or two eight-by-ten glossy photographs of the speaker—that's it. With a bureau, the glossies come with two or three publicity pictures, a biographical sketch, other important information regarding past speaking engagements, and usually a press release that can be used as is. All of this is *very* helpful.

Third, they are helpful troubleshooters. They will give advice if you ask for it and often have a wealth of ideas to share. They have probably worked on twice as many events as anyone in your Friends group, they know what works and what doesn't, and they can help make the event most enjoyable for the speaker and successful for the group. This is especially true when the speaker's agenda for the big day is drawn up. The bureau representatives will remind organizers that the speaker needs some rest before the event and suggest other considerations that might cause problems if overlooked.

# AGENTS

Agents usually don't present the same problems as speaker's bureaus. An agent will, if time allows, have the speaker talk directly with the Friends representative when the occasion demands it. Otherwise the agent takes down a request on Monday and calls the Friends representative back on Tuesday with a response.

Whether the speaker uses a bureau or an agent, try to make *initial* contact directly with the speaker. If a potential speaker contacted refers you to a bureau, the Friends group really doesn't have much say in the matter. Making that initial contact, however, may provide an added edge and may even entice the speaker to sign on without the bureau.

# SETTING THE DATE

The specific date for your event must be negotiated, but bear in mind that the invited speaker is doing the Friends a favor unless he or she is hungry for work or loves speaking to groups. More often than not, the chosen speaker will have selected your invitation out of a number of other options because it is an intriguing offer. But his or her schedule may leave few open dates from which you must choose.

On the other hand, do not accept a time when virtually everyone in town will be out, or when the event would coincide with another major community event. Previous contact with other civic groups, churches and synagogues, and the local chamber of commerce should make it possible to choose a date that is virtually conflict-free.

In the invitation, suggest several possible dates and times. Also let the speaker know which dates will not work at all. For example, your invitation might suggest a time in the fall. When the speaker accepts, the specific time in the fall can then be negotiated.

It is fine to send as many as a half-dozen letters to potential speakers simultaneously. If you are writing to nationally known speakers, answers to invitations could be three to six weeks in coming. It isn't necessary to mail all six the same day, or even the same week. Mailing a few one week and a few the next seems to be adequate. Should the unlikely occur and two speakers respond positively, you could always ask one to speak at a later event.

# SELECTING A SITE

Once the date is chosen, the table and accommodations committees will need to line up an appropriate site for your event. The size of your anticipated audience is the key factor. Select a site that will seat about one-half to two-thirds of the expected audience. Even if chairs must be added along with meals and tables, or people must be turned away, the impression left will be one of a sellout. Do not choose a facility that will dwarf a small audience. In this case, smaller is better. At the same time, be sure not to cramp the diners. People get hostile when they must eat elbow to elbow, so it's best to put people around a table that will allow for adequate eating space.

The chosen site must be reasonably accessible. There must be adequate parking, and people must be able to leave their cars with the assurance that those cars will be there, hubcaps and all, when they return. Scout the neighborhood, even to the extent of asking the local authorities what sort of vandalism record the area has. Failure to do this, and the subsequent report of hubcaps missing or tires slashed, will only hurt the program.

Adequate parking should also mean that patrons do not have to walk more than two blocks from their cars. Longer distances than this will mean patrons complaining that they nearly died "hiking" to the dinner from the neighboring county. This also makes it difficult for the disabled to attend.

Members of the table and accommodations committee should also check out the building for wheelchair accessibility. If the building does not have ramps or other similar accommodations, and they cannot be provided, then select another site or announce in the publicity that the event could not be made wheelchair-accessible.

# CHOOSING A MENU

Selecting the dinner menu may be the second most important aspect of planning your annual dinner event, second only to choosing the speaker. Committee members may believe that they can scrimp and save on the dinner, but try to remember that no matter what is charged for the dinner, it will be considered too much by at least half of the audience. Also, remember the last time *you* went out for some sort of cultural gathering where food was served. Did *you* complain about the rubber chicken or the cold fish? If so, why do it to your patrons?

Eye appeal is essential for a meal, and it is a good idea to choose a meal that is colorful as well as good. If working with an on-campus cafeteria, have them make several of the dinners and try them out before ordering one for the event. If the dinner is catered, ask for samples. There shouldn't be a charge for this. If there is, get another caterer. Asking someone to buy food they haven't tasted is like trying to sell a car without a test-drive.

Work with the chef or caterer, but don't be cowed by him or her. Ask to see a full range of what they are capable of doing with a per-plate cost. This information is necessary in order to figure out what must be charged to cover costs and still raise funds. This cannot be done without some figuring. While this sort of figuring is a lot like economic forecasting, a "ballpark" figure for what is affordable is at least possible.

For example, add together the costs of the meal, publicity, hall rental (unless it's taking place on campus or is free), hotel, air transportation, amenities, and decorations from the budget work-sheet (Figure 6-1). This amount, plus the cost for the speaker, gives you the amount you think it will cost you to host the event. Divide this number by a *conservative* estimate of the number of people you think will attend, and you have about what you can afford per plate and still see a profit. In the sample, the estimated costs were about $24 per person. It was determined that we simply could not go above $25 per plate, so we took a chance. As it turned out, our costs were lower and our profit therefore was higher. One assumption being made here is that the Friends account shows zero. For most Friends groups organizing a first event, established funding is simply not there. Keeping costs low is, of course, a high priority. Of course, if the event is successful, there should be some funding for the next annual event.

How do you arrive at the right price to charge for the dinner? By talking with the caterer or dining hall personnel. Begin with the cheapest price offered and move up. If $6 a plate gets you a fish stick, a salad, and a vegetable, ask about the $6.50 meal, and so on. By mixing meat and vegetables (for example, beef tips over rice), one can find a very appetizing meal for a relatively low price, allowing for a higher profit margin. Whatever is decided, remember the advice about making the meal eye-appealing. Since eating healthy is much in vogue, vegetarian-type meals may also prove cost-effective.

# CHOOSING A THEME

The table arrangements committee should realize that nothing can brighten a place up like some well-placed centerpieces and tablecloths. One year, when our annual event had to be postponed until December because of our speaker's schedule, we used red tablecloths and white napkins. The dining hall was decorated in sparse but highly visible Christmas colors. The tables had garlands of holly and pinecones, with green or white candles alternating on each of the tables. The first impression one had upon entering the room was breathtaking.

Another year our Friends group made 600 fall-colored napkin rings. At all six of our annual Friends dinners, we always had a large centerpiece at the head table, using some fresh flowers or a silk arrangement. The silk arrangements were later used in the library. Each table also had a smaller centerpiece in keeping with the theme chosen. We made it a point to offer the smaller centerpieces for sale to those seated at the tables. We usually sold 80 percent of all the arrangements the night of the dinner.

With the help of the executive board, the table arrangements committee should choose a motif that is in concert with the event.

In our case, the decorations produced ample town talk for a few weeks after each event. All of the dinner speakers commented, without prompting, about our group's stunning table arrangements. One speaker apparently did our publicity for us. When we contacted another speaker a few years later, he *already* knew of these dinners in a small Tennessee town because he had heard about them from a previous speaker!

# PUBLICITY

Advertising for the event can never begin too early, and this should be stressed over and over again to the publicity committee. It *must* begin as soon as the speaker and the date of the event is known. If the local press cooperates, and the speaker is noteworthy, hold a press conference to announce the event.

Use publicity to draw specific audiences. For example, I had an associate who had been a mainstay at our college for more than a quarter of a century, had worked with children, had a very strong interest in children's literature, and was something of a children's writer herself. She suggested that we hold a poster contest for children in the area to publicize the children's writer we invited one year. The program was a wonderful success. The speaker judged the winning entries and posed for photographs with each winner and a group portrait. The children also received one free ticket to the dinner. Because publicity is so important, the next chapter covers this topic in detail.

## SPECIAL INVITATIONS FOR SPECIAL GUESTS

It's the details that can provide the competitive edge in the Friends business. While it may be a cliche, it is nevertheless true that details often make a difference. Invitations are a case in point. The temptation is to think that preprinted invitations are fine. Just get one and send it and get on to other business. Don't let the publicity committee fall victim to this kind of erroneous thinking.

Special guests need special attention. By working with others on the board or Friends committees, a group of one, two, or three dozen individuals who need special care may be identified. Send these guests special printed invitations. This might be politicians, power brokers not involved with the Friends, or others. Devise an invitation that will grab attention, elegantly invite, and leave a lasting impression.

These people are merely being invited to come; they are not being offered a free ride. The invitation should have on it some indication of where tickets may be purchased. While some may consider this advice elitist, it has been found to be very beneficial wherever it has been tried.

## THE PRESS

The press is an enigma that can greatly aid the annual event or completely hamstring it. Working with the press can be like learning how to handle a porcupine. Thankfully, this is not always true.

In small towns, the press is usually run by a handful of people: one for the paper, one for radio, and one for television. It may even be the same family who runs them all. In slightly larger towns, more outlets will mean more people, but clearly only a few owners will dominate.

If the relationship with the press has been established as outlined in chapter 2, the publicity committee will not be making contact for the first time. If good contact has been maintained all year, the press will react to the program far more favorably than if you suddenly call one afternoon and announce, "You need to get a reporter out here tonight to cover our library event." Establish contact early on, since Friends news will probably be of marginal interest to the community. The press know this, and they can always say the magic word "space" or "time" to excuse themselves from printing a story. The carefully built press relationship will obviate this excuse in many cases.

## PREPARING FOR THE SPEAKER'S ARRIVAL

The accommodations committee should plan to spend more than is entirely necessary on hotel accommodations for the speaker. Members should think of the place where they would like to stay and then go one better. This will always pay off, even if it means paying ten or fifteen dollars more. The speaker needs to have pleasant memories of the visit. *Always* check the rooms out, or have another member of the accommodations committee check them out. Be sure to have the charges for the room prearranged with the hotel to prevent any embarrassment.

About three months before the speaker arrives, someone on the program committee needs to spend some time each week researching the speaker's background, likes and dislikes, and above all, anything and everything he or she has written. If possible, the committee member who will introduce the speaker at the dinner should read as many of the speaker's works as possible before the speaker arrives.

If it is not possible to read all the author's works, choose the most recent three to five works. Be sure to read both the works, the criticisms of the works, and the reviews. Always try to find unfavorable as well as favorable reviews. This will create the impression that you have done your homework. Speakers like nothing less than to go to a place where it is painfully obvious no one has prepared for their arrival. One speaker remarked to the author that it was refreshing to be at a place where, at long last, the person in charge had actually read her books!

As mentioned earlier in this chapter, good publicity is essential to the success of the annual event. Because publicity is the Friends group's voice in the outside world, the next chapter will be devoted to the agony and the ecstasy of working with the press and getting out publicity.

# THINGS TO DO

1. Using *Current Biography* and other similar sources (*Biography Index*, etc.), have a member of the program committee make a list of speakers that would "mesh" well with the program. Addresses may be found in current *Who's Who* editions and other standard reference sources.

2. Call Friends of Libraries USA and ask them for the names of some Friends groups that have used dinners as main events. Also, ask them for the names of libraries that have used other types of annual get-togethers.

3. Take this list and present it to the executive board. Get their reactions to the proposed potential speakers. Remember to have background information about each one in case there are those who know nothing about them. Leave the meeting with at least five names of potential speakers.

4. Draft an invitation letter with the program director to send to each member. Review it with all or most of the executive board members for criticisms and comments.

5. Ask a disinterested third party to read the letter. Then ask the following questions:

   *What* is being asked?
   *When* (time and date) is the event scheduled?
   *What* is expected?
   *Where* is the addressee going?
   *To whom* does the addressee reply?
   When satisfied with your letter, assemble a simple packet of materials. Mail the finished product.

6. If your list of potential names of speakers is exhausted, call a speaker's bureau and ask for a list of its speakers. Be sure to ask them to include price ranges. This is not a commitment to use. If, however, you want to call one of the speakers listed, chances are he or she will be accessible only through that bureau. Talk with experienced Friends organizers on the difference between working directly with the speaker or with a bureau. Jot down the names of bureaus that are highly recommended.

7. Meet with the executive board and decide on a general time—such as fall or spring. Once this has been decided, and the speaker has been invited, begin thinking about motifs.

8. Check with local arrangers to see how they can help. Be sure to examine all possibilities and not just the major florists in the area.

9. Is there any talent in this area already on board? Is someone good at crafts? If so, ask them to plan the motif for the group.

10. Get a list of at least a dozen (if possible) hotel accommodations with prices and room types. Ask about discounts and other benefits that might help save the Friends money.

11. Check with local printers about printed invitations. Be sure to see if they will make this part of their community donation to the event.

12. Call the local newspaper. Ask if they would allow a Friends member to write a story about the speaker for publication. Often they will, if it is well-written. Be sure to include a photograph and try to connect the speaker's topic with local events.

# 7 PUBLICIZING YOUR PROGRAM

Abraham Lincoln once said, "With public sentiment, nothing can fail; without it nothing can succeed." Lincoln was right, of course. Nothing is more inimical to a successful Friends group than failed public sentiment. The work of the Friends group, through the publicity committee, is to weave a magic spell, to cast the net of influence over people and pull them in. Understanding this is easy; doing it is much harder.

## PUBLICITY: HOW NECESSARY IS IT?

Is publicity really all that necessary? Consider for a moment that the users of the library, whether it is a public, academic, or special library, are but one part of a larger community. If all patrons could be counted on to attend a given library function, then advertising to them alone would be sufficient. But because only about 25 percent of everyone who reads the notices will actually *consider* attending, and of those considering, about a quarter of them will actually attend, it is necessary to reach beyond the library to the entire community.

The publicity committee's areas of concern should include the following: newsletters, small groups, civic and parochial organizations, educational organizations, print media, television and radio media, special groups, and, lastly, "scattershot" advertising. Whether you choose to focus on all of these areas or only some of them will be determined by how much you want to succeed. If you or anyone on your publicity committee feels skittish about publicizing the library or your Friends program, then the rest of this chapter may be hard to take. Rather than resisting these suggestions, try losing your skittishness by concentrating on how much more will be available to students and patrons if your Friends event is successful.

## NEWSLETTERS

We have already discussed newsletters to some extent, but they are worth mentioning again. Whether one, four, or 52 newsletters a year are published, be aware of how important this vehicle is for the publicity campaign. Once the event is planned, don't hesitate to talk about it in the newsletter, *early on*—months ahead of time. But mention it on any page other than the front page. Closer to the event, you can devote the front page of the newsletter, and possibly the entire newsletter, to the event.

# SMALL GROUPS AND PAROCHIAL GROUPS

Small groups such as garden clubs, social or athletic clubs, church groups, and other similar organizations can be important contacts for your publicity efforts.

Remember the early chapters about visiting these groups? Has it been done? If so, it will be quite natural to call on them now. Draft a brief letter to the president of a given civic group telling him or her about the upcoming event. The letter might begin by mentioning your last meeting (if you had one) and its nature. Suppose the last visit involved attending another civic program together. A letter addressed to the civic officer might read, "While that program was exciting, I think I have one equally exciting for you, and one that I am most enthusiastic about." Then go on to describe the program and solicit the club's help.

The final paragraph will tell what the officer can do: advertise the Friends program. Ask if you can send a news release, request the group's mailing list, offer to speak to the group, and send copies of your newsletter for each member (the one that carries the front page story about the annual event), or all of the above. The more you do, the more your potential audience will increase. Speak before these groups if possible. Better still, offer to speak to them long *before* the Friends group is under way. By doing this, you will set a precedent, and the library's services will be well-known to the group. Speaking to the group does all involved a favor.

The executive board might want to consider whether or not the Friends group can afford to offer a discount to the group's members, especially if they fill a table. If they do, offer to recognize them at the dinner. Since these groups need the publicity too, they will jump at the chance. If time allows at the dinner, mention a word or two about the civic groups attending the annual event.

Small group advertising pays by establishing the Friends group as a leader of other groups. By working cooperatively with other groups, participative management is extended beyond the library's walls, and beyond the small confines of the Friends group. Soon after this, the dividends will be obvious: consultation with other groups, speaking engagements, collaborative associations, and more.

With parochial groups, personal contact is necessary. This will probably mean going by a church or synagogue one day during office hours and talking with a pastor, a priest, a rabbi, or a director of religious education. The visit need not be long. Be sure to call ahead of time for an appointment, and make certain to limit the visit to no longer than *fifteen minutes*. It is essential to leave them written information. Try to leave at least one or two posters, one news release, and a couple of newsletters. This will prove an excellent way of alerting the community to the Friends event.

Many parochial groups will also have a newsletter for their members. This is also a good way to expand publicity for the event. A short paragraph, a catchy line or two, or even a sentence will return several "takers" to your event.

Getting into churches' or synagogues' bulletins can be difficult since space is limited and generally reserved for their own activities. Some places of worship have schools attached to them, while others sponsor worthy community projects. Make sure when you talk with a minister, priest, or rabbi that you discuss all the different organizations within that place of worship: adult groups, women's groups, young adult groups. If he or she agrees to put up a poster, so much the better. If not, leave it anyway. A place may be found for it later.

# CIVIC GROUPS

Advertising to civic groups such as the Rotary, Lions, and Kiwanis clubs should be done early and often. Civic groups are usually well organized and set meetings months in advance. Again, offer to speak to these groups, and when you do, talk about the library and its plans. If possible, try to get on the speaking circuit with one of these clubs. For example, the Friends leader or the librarian could offer to speak on library-related issues and problems.

More important than speaking and advertising, however, is the power these groups possess. Generally, community leaders belong to these clubs, serving on various committees. The sooner you get to know them, the better off the Friends group will be. Spend some time lunching with members of these groups whenever possible, and invite them to the library for different events, however small they might be.

Civic groups often have some means of communication with their members. Many have a monthly one-page newsletter. Make certain the Friends program is listed in their newsletters. Often this will be no more than one sentence or a few lines. Every notice, however, means more exposure.

Don't forget that these organizations also have national offices. Often, if the Friends program showcases an important topic or speaker, mention will be made in the national newsletter of these organizations. This will do little for attendance locally, but it may help later with other programs. The more people there are who know about your Friends group, the more people you will have at the annual event. At several Friends dinners my library hosted, visitors from as far away as 200 miles attended, their presence often the direct result of outside advertising.

Keep in mind, too, that each person in the Lions, Rotary, or Kiwanis clubs represents *some* business. Maybe one member is the CEO of a local corporation, is a doctor, or is a lawyer in town. Be sure to make these contacts and ask if there is some in-house publication in which advertising could be placed for their employees.

Friends groups in public libraries will also want to remember to advertise in city government publications. This is not to say that Friends groups of academic libraries could not do the same, but public libraries are an arm of the city government. Some city governments might be shy to advertise a program for a local *private* college, but they would probably jump at the chance to advertise what the local public library is doing to help improve library service to the community.

# EDUCATIONAL ORGANIZATIONS

Educational organizations, including elementary and secondary schools, colleges and universities, PTAs and PTOs, and other educational groups growing out of parent-school partnerships offer many opportunities to reach an important audience. Of course, young school children will probably not attend the Friends program unless it is one that is geared to their interests, but their parents might. Because colleges and universities have the families of their students already committed to supporting their programs, academic Friends groups may have a somewhat easier time plugging into a ready-made audience.

Contact the schools in surrounding cities, townships, and suburbs. Visit the principals and talk with them. Get the names of the officers of the parents' group, and take several posters and flyers to them. Be sure, of course, to visit the school librarian. If nothing else, posters and flyers can go up in the faculty lounge or the school library. If you have extra copies of your newsletter, leave several in the faculty lounges, the school library, and of course one with the principal. Be sure to ask the principals if their schools publish a newsletter that goes home to parents. If they do—and many schools have them—try to get into the issue that comes out nearest to the date of the event.

For the schools you cannot visit, send a letter of introduction with some flyers and, if affordable, one or two posters. Principals get more mail than they have time to set fire to, but experience indicates that they always like to know of good educational programs in the community. If principals in the area are unlikely to respond to letters, send them to the school librarian.

For the parents' groups (the PTA and PTO), a letter should suffice. Somewhere in the letter, request that they mention the Friends event in any "Calendar of Events" they maintain. This letter, as with most others, should be one page in length and should include, either at the top or bottom, a contact name, an address, and a phone number where at least one Friends member could be reached at night. If your word processing capabilities permit, position this contact name in bold print, set off from the rest of the letter.

Materials sent to colleges and universities should be addressed either to the Office of Public Affairs, the Office of Communications, the Office of Personnel, or to the president of the institution. The same letter should also be sent to the college or university librarian. If in doubt, contact the librarian and ask for the name and appropriate office to which such notices should be sent. In some cases, the librarian may be willing to run interference. At the very least, he or she should put up a few posters and/or flyers.

In the letter to the person in charge of community and campus events, indicate the purpose of the event, include some flyers and a poster, and ask that a notice be inserted in any campus-wide mailings. Leave a few newsletters in the faculty lounge, the library, the student center, or all three. Faculty at colleges and universities are most likely to be interested in such programs, so advertise widely on campuses. Again, discounts for faculty who come in groups large enough to occupy at least one table should be considered. *Any* group that cannot fill up at least *one* table should not receive discounted tickets.

If you offer discounted tickets for only partially filled tables, you'll end up with many tables only half-full. Discounted tickets should be offered in numbers divisible by the number it takes to fill a table completely. This does not mean that if eight seats fill a table, and the Lions Club wants ten, that it is turned away. Simply explain that while one table will be reserved, the other two people will have to fend for themselves.

If possible, the Friends leader or the librarian should find a forum at which to give a brief commercial about the upcoming event (such as a faculty meeting). If this cannot be arranged, be sure areas that are frequented by faculty, staff, and students (mailroom, student center, cafeteria) are well-papered with flyers and/or posters. Expect stiff competition for bulletin board space, but whatever space is available will be seen by *someone*. Again, *exposure* of the program is what you want. The more people are exposed to advertising in advance, the larger the audience will be the night of the event.

Other educational organizations might include music or reading groups, current events discussion groups, small group clubs in colleges and universities, film societies, and theatre groups.

# THE PRESS

If at this point Friends personnel are just getting around to introducing themselves to the media, the media may be unresponsive. If a relationship already has been established, chances are they will be ready to help. Of course, if one member of the publicity committee or executive board is also a member of the press, so much the better. No matter what, the media may still resort to the old excuse: "We haven't enough time to air it." (The newspaper version of this is, "We haven't the space to run it.")

There aren't many ways to get around the media, especially if they are entrenched as a monopoly handling print, radio, and television in the area. What works is persistence. Use members from the board or influential Friends to make calls to the press. The important point is to keep calling them, provide them with news releases, and try to find higher-ups who will wield more power than the local news reporter who may not have time for the Friends group. It also helps if you can deliver news copy directly to the station or newspaper, complete with photographs of the speaker and a few words about the event.

## THE PRESS RELEASE

When you send a press release, head the page, in all capital letters, PRESS RELEASE. A few lines down from the top, on the left or right side of the page, put the words "For Immediate Release" or "For Release . . ." and the date (if the news is to be held until a certain date). Never send an announcement more than a week before its release date.

Remember the journalism major's five Ws: Who, What, When, Where, and Why. The first sentence of the release should state these five important facts. In the body of the release, talk about other matters that are of importance but may not be part of the five Ws formula. Releases should be double-spaced and should not exceed one page. The closing of the release can include a tag phrase such as, "For more information on tickets, ticket discounts, and group rates, call . . ."

## FOLLOW-UP

After the press release has been sent, follow up with a call to the contact reporter to see if the press release is sufficient, or if there are any articles someone in the Friends group could write about the speaker or the event. If the contact can write an article about the event, offer to supply whatever background is needed.

If the reporter needs additional information, you could create a brief fact sheet with headings on the left side of the sheet and information on the right side. The headings for a speaker fact sheet might be: Biographical Information, Accomplishments, Current Work, and Future Plans. You also could send the Friends of the Library newsletter and highlight the pertinent facts. Or, a Friends member could write a feature story and you could "pitch it" to a reporter. Whatever you provide for the reporter should be brief but substantial.

Once you "place" your story with a newspaper or radio or TV station, it's a good idea to take both the organization's head person and the reporter out to lunch and talk over strategy. This may not prove helpful immediately, but it will later. During lunch, talk about whatever else the Friends group can offer them. Radio station managers are always looking for filler air time. Could someone in the Friends group plug new books or relate an interesting story for that day or week in history? The same could be done for the newspaper. For television, recommend community experts or good books on topics of local concern. If the Friends group is attached to an academic library, recommend faculty who can speak authoritatively on newsworthy topics.

## PUBLIC SERVICE ANNOUNCEMENTS

All radio and television stations are required to run public service announcements (PSAs), but not necessarily from your Friends group. Remember, a PSA does not have to have visuals even on television. It can be read over the air during a station's usual "Community Calendar" segment. Be sure to mark the *outside* of the envelope "PSA" or "Public Service Announcement." This will prevent the Friends group from being charged for the spot, and will also help to put it in the right hands. Because public service announcements are free, they should be sent no less than four weeks in advance.

Include in the PSA the same information you provided in the press release, but in an abbreviated form. Once your PSAs are out, alert the Friends membership to listen for them. Do this to be sure the announcement gets on the air—and that the wrong information is not aired.

## SURVIVING FRUSTRATION WITH THE MEDIA

Working with the media can be a very frustrating experience. But whatever the source of your frustration, always remember that it *can* be overcome. Some situations will be very real, legitimate problems that cannot be circumvented. Those must be endured. Others may be political or ideological. Those have to be overcome. This is why it is important to begin media relationships early on and try to find whatever possible obstacles may be lurking in the way *before* they stymie publicity for the Friends event. Generally, even major rifts that have occurred in the past between the library and the media can be repaired. It is a good idea, however, to check out the library's past media relations before plunging in.

# SPECIAL GROUP PUBLICITY

Special group publicity refers to announcing your event to such groups as trustees, administrators, faculty members, library boards, and governing bodies. All of these groups are important, though not always essential as an audience for the annual event. Be sure, however, that they get some information about the event. It's surprising how helpful this can be. In my library, we did this every year for four years, with no return on effort. The fifth year, however, one trustee (who lived in another state) liked the speaker so much that he underwrote all of our speaker's costs. So, one publicity letter netted us about $8,000!

The crazy thing about publicizing these events is that you don't know which outlet will produce the right mix of people to make the event successful until after the event. And sometimes it changes from year to year. It is best to try to hit as many of these groups as possible to ensure adequate coverage.

Other special groups will emerge as you examine your own community, library, and Friends group. Obviously, it will be necessary to use the Friends membership liberally, not only calling on it to help with publicizing the annual event (no one person, or even four or five people can do all this), but also asking for contacts members may have that have been overlooked. These special groups should be pursued as carefully as any of the other groups mentioned previously.

# SCATTERSHOT ADVERTISING

Scattershot advertising refers to posters and flyers that are displayed wherever large numbers of people will see them, such as malls, large grocery stores, and other places where people in the community are likely to gather. Once again, knowing the community is important. If you take the time to ferret out these places in advance, you'll know which ones to use when you're ready to advertise your Friends program.

We live in a mall age. In small towns malls are hangouts for everyone from young kids (who go there to spend their parents' hard-earned money) to elderly couples. Placing several posters at strategic points, and then taking a few flyers to some of the larger stores, will prove very helpful.

Grocery stores, especially the large ones, are also very useful. Managers are usually generous with space, and they will often allow a poster of some size to be placed in a heavily trafficked area. Getting a poster into every store or mall in a large town, is, of course, impractical. But you should at least make every effort to publicize the event in the vicinity of the group's outreach.

Posters should be about 10 by 20 inches. Bright pastel colors, even Day-Glo colors, are very good eye-grabbers. These can be cheaply printed from camera-ready copy that you and your publicity committee have put together. Almost any craft store will have the necessary lettering. With advice from committee members, design the poster, glue on the letters, and have it run off.

The poster, as well as the flyer, should have the group's name followed by "presents" and the speaker's name. Below that should be the time, the place, and the date. Any ticket information should go at the bottom of the poster, either on the left or right side, and contact information should be on the opposite side. Make sure the poster is not too busy; include just enough to tell people what they need to know in order to come.

Try the poster out on committee members. Before taking it to a printer, give it a trial run. Have someone unfamiliar with the poster walk by it. Ask them the five Ws: who, what, when, where, and why. If they can't answer all of them, something has probably been left out. If they have to stop to read it, it's probably too wordy.

# THINGS TO DO

1. Go to the local craft shop and get the things necessary for a poster: poster board (three sheets), lettering, glue (if not self-adhesive), and tape.

2. Contact the civic groups in the area to see what avenues they use for publicity.

3. Put together a poster and examine it for readability.

4. Distribute the posters and flyers to churches, colleges or universities, large civic groups, and place them in strategic areas around town. Ask for advice about where the posters should go from committee members.

5. Contact the local radio stations, especially the public stations. Set up a time to go by and talk with them about the event.

6. Call a press conference and announce the particulars about the event.

7. Call the local newspaper(s). Ask reporters if someone can come by and talk with them about an upcoming newsworthy event. Offer a feature story to the local newspaper on the coming Friends event.

8. Examine "your own backyard" to be sure you haven't left out any publicity avenues within your own facility.

# 8 MAKING ARRANGEMENTS

Planning is the basic building block of the Friends group. When arrangements are made for an annual event and something is overlooked, *everyone* in attendance notices. The awful thing about arrangements is that it's usually the obvious thing that's left undone. Imagine this scenario: It's the day of the event and everything appears in place. The speaker is retrieved from the airport and whisked off to the hotel. "Egad! The hotel! I forget to get the speaker a hotel room!"

There are steps you can follow that will help you avoid missing the obvious. The most important arrangements you have to make are for the speaker, the speech, the audience, the tables, and special events. Let's look at each one of these and see what's involved.

## ARRANGEMENTS FOR THE SPEAKER

Arrangements for the speaker will begin as soon as the contract is signed and a copy is kept for the Friends records. If the speaker does not furnish a contract, the Program Committee should have one drawn up for legal protection. The contract does not need to be elaborate, but it should include when and how much the speaker is to be paid and what the speaker will do for the money. Most contracts call for half the payment before the event and the other half immediately afterward.

### FLIGHTS

For most speakers traveling long distances, you will need to make flight arrangements. (The main exception is if the speaker is a veteran of the speaking circuit, in which case these arrangements will be made by his or her office.) Both the program committee and the Friends leader need to know when the speaker will arrive in town. Before the contract was signed, the program committee chair and the Friends leader worked what they hoped the speaker would agree to do (attend a reception, hold a press conference, tape a commercial for a local charity) and put this in the contract agreement. The next step is to draw up an itinerary for the speaker to follow while in town.

Once the itinerary is set, the program committee chair or the Friends leader (it should be the same person each time) should call the speaker (or the speaker's bureau) to discuss the travel schedule and arrangements. Flight connections to small towns are notoriously difficult. Be sure to plan for this problem if your local airport is small or hard to get to.

If the airport is too small for comfortable connections, try to find a hub as close to the town as possible. Perhaps one is only 50 or 100 miles away. Could someone from the arrangements committee drive the distance in an hour or two and get the speaker into town much earlier than waiting for the last flight into town? This means extra work, but it might save you from a nervous breakdown as you wait for the plane to arrive.

## PRESS INTERVIEW

Arrange, if possible, to have a brief press conference at the airport, especially if the speaker arrives the day before the event. Six o'clock news coverage the day before the event might even add a dozen or so more guests. At the very least, some sort of quasi-formal welcome to the city is in order. Perhaps the mayor, the president of the college, or a trustee of the public library could give an award, make a presentation, or say a few words of welcome. By welcoming the speaker immediately and with news coverage, the speaker will feel he or she has agreed to attend a first-rate event.

Another, longer press interview may be held prior to the dinner. For this event, have a room set up with a one-page sheet identifying the speaker and something about him or her, some water for the speaker, and plenty of outlets for cameras and recorders.

If a press conference is held immediately before the dinner, a fact sheet on the speaker should be placed on a table for reporters. Someone, most likely the Friends leader or the chair of the publicity committee, should be prepared to field questions, starting from right to left. The speaker may do this, but someone should be prepared to do it in case the speaker does not take charge. If questions and answers are allowed after the speaker's address is over, the Friends leader or someone else involved with the group should field the questions.

## HOTEL ACCOMMODATIONS

The speaker must also have hotel accommodations. These should be made weeks ahead of time. Be sure someone checks the hotel room ahead of time. It's a nice touch if you can have it spruced up with fruit and flowers. Usually fruit baskets and cut flowers cost very little. Speakers *will* notice these amenities! Adding that something extra to the speaker's room shows special attention and will make the speaker feel at home.

**TRANSPORTATION: TO AND FROM**

You will also need to make arrangements for transportation. My own Friends group was very lucky in this regard. We never paid full price for any limousine service. Town patrons provided it in full, or at least at half-price. Our printer often supplied a nice car, or we borrowed one from an affluent patron. To go to these extra lengths helps to create an image. Sure, the speaker can be transported in a station wagon that the children have made a playroom out of, but why not make the extra effort? Usually, if a Friends member with a nice car is asked to do the transporting, he or she will jump at the chance to be privy to the conversation of so important a guest.

# ARRANGEMENTS FOR THE SPEECH

Arrangements for the speech begin with checking the acoustics of the hall. Before doing this, however, check with the speaker to find out if the speech may be taped. A tape of the speech would make an excellent addition to the library's holdings, but do not assume that taping is customary. Many speakers have contracts that strictly prohibit any taping that is not cleared through the bureau's or the speaker's office. If the address is taped unlawfully, the library, the Friends group, and the speaker could be in for some rough sailing. If a problem of this nature occurs, a letter usually is sufficient to clear things up.

Checking out the acoustics of a hall is best accomplished by having someone speak in a normal voice over the amplification system. Have several people positioned in four or five places in the hall to see if what is being said is clearly audible. If in some part of the hall a "dead" area is found, ask the owners what can be done to improve it (especially if you are expecting any hard-of-hearing patrons to attend the event). If nothing can be done, make a note of the area and do not place tables there. Remember that if the acoustics are bad without people in the hall, they will not be improved with several hundred bodies added.

It's also important to think about backup amplification in case the main system fails. Don't rely on a "fail-safe" system that has been in service for 100 years without a hitch. It is sure to fail the night of the annual event if backup amplification is not ready. It's a good idea to have the person in charge of the speaking system have a backup taping system ready, too.

The speaking arrangements should also include special information to the press, sent weeks before the event. This may indicate times for interviews, press conference information, and so forth. It does not have to include a copy of the speaker's address, but this might be requested. If a copy is not available, have a short synopsis prepared based on your conversations with the speaker.

## HEAD TABLES

Arrangements for the speech should also include planning the head table. The first order of business is whether or not to have one. Some will no doubt object to a head table as the height of arrogance and elitism. This is a silly charge. A head table honors those who have worked themselves silly for the event, or have paid a sizable amount to see that "the show goes on." A head table can be a very useful addition. It also serves to focus attention to one point in the room.

In an academic setting, the head table will nearly always include the president of the college or university, the vice-president, the library director, the associate librarian, the speaker, spouses, and, of course, the Friends leader. In a public library, trustees replace college officials, the mayor replaces the college or university president, and the rest are the same. Most etiquette books explain where to seat persons at this table.

The division of labor at the table is easily meted out. In an academic setting, the president of the college or university introduces the program and welcomes the audience. The Friends leader (or library director) introduces the speaker and makes some closing remarks. The vice president introduces the head table and any special guests in the audience. Of course, the division of labor does not have to be this exact, but some type of delegation is necessary so that one or two people are not talking the entire evening. The Friends leader should also auction off the centerpieces on the tables, if any are used, at the end of the dinner.

## LENGTH OF ADDRESS

You should talk with the speaker weeks or even months ahead of time about how long the speech will be. Of course, as the featured entertainment of the night, the speaker may take as long as he or she wants. But any speaker who wants to talk for more than 60 minutes had better be exceptional. It is more likely that your speaker will want to speak for about 40 minutes, in which case you must allocate the remaining time for the other speakers. *Do not* assume that presidents and vice-presidents, trustees, or even library directors will know how long "a few minutes" are when told. Tell them to speak no more than five minutes, or whatever amount is appropriate. It is a good idea to ask them what they intend to say. This may prove difficult if the president never prepares such remarks until about ten minutes before giving them, as some are wont to do.

## POLITICS OF ACADEMIC LIBRARIES

The very setting—many potential donors to the library, the college, the special audience, captive for the moment—will prove a temptation irresistible for some presidents of colleges or universities. This is exactly what is *not* wanted. Make sure no one is "two-timing" the Friends group by soliciting funds for the college by passing out materials as the audience leaves.

The Friends leader should also time his or her remarks (if he or she does not give way to the library director on this occasion). The Friends leader may be up at the podium for a while at the end of the event auctioning off table arrangements, but be sure comments about the Friends group and the library in general are not more than 15 minutes. Bear in mind that the audience has had a full meal, is groggy from its consumption, has already listened to three or four people talk, and is now ready to go home. The worst-case scenario would be for the Friends leader to talk for a half-hour, only to see half the audience leave after 15 minutes.

## DON'T FORGET TO SAY "THANK YOU"

Arrangements for the speech also mean making public thank-yous. Plot this carefully and well. A general "heartfelt thank-you to all of those who helped" will not do. Take a few moments a day or two before the dinner and jot down the names of those who helped with the event. Remember to thank even those who were paid for a service, if the service was rendered at less than the market price. In-kind contributions also need to be acknowledged.

This should *not* result in a list of four dozen names. If it does, see if some can be combined. If several work for the same company, thank the company. Publicity for these companies makes owners happy and may encourage others to help.

## THE AUDIENCE AND THE TABLES

Arrangements for the audience begin with the tickets for the event. Of all the "little" things to do, this can create the most confusion. The first issue to settle is whether or not the committee will mail tickets to those who phone for them. Tickets should be mailed out, but watch the following provisos. Be sure to tell all callers that the tickets will not be mailed *until* the check is received. In the envelope that is mailed back, be sure to include a receipt. Since postal costs have increased so dramatically over the years, and service has diminished at an equally dramatic pace, cut off all mailing seven working days before the event.

Patrons who call should be warned that tickets will be mailed out no later than seven working days before the event. This may seem excessive to some, but in rural areas, some post offices send mail to a regional collection center 100 miles away. If promises are made too close to the day of the event, logistical problems will mount.

A *short* letter should accompany the tickets (mainly to provide cover for them through the mail). The letter should outline the cost, the event, and the time and place. The tickets should be about one inch by three inches. The ticket should have the Friends group's name on it, the name of the event, the speaker, the time, the place, and the cost.

Tickets mean keeping a book of reservations. This can be confusing. The first thing to remember is to keep only *one* book. Let any library staff member or any arrangements committee member take ticket orders, but have only *one* number to call for tickets. Use an accounting book or some other book that comes with lines for entries and columns for labeling. (See the sample in Figure 8-1.) For our event, we kept one book that was sectioned off into the following columns: name, phone number, address, number of tickets, paid or not, date mailed, and amount received. *All* of these columns are important and should be used. The names and addresses are not only important for getting the tickets to the right person, but for adding to the Friends mailing list later.

The ticket book should be kept as neat as possible. All that is needed for pandemonium to occur is to have tickets going to Smiths instead of the Smits.

Those ordering less than seven days before the event should be placed near the end of the book for easy reference (unless earlier calls turn up with unpaid tickets). Unmailed tickets should be placed in individual small envelopes with the name of the person on the outside and the amount due under the name. This way the tickets *and* how much is owed is all in one place.

No system is foolproof, however. Invariably, one or two angry patrons will storm the head table moments before the event begins, asking why their tickets are not ready. If patrons are vociferous about having paid, let them in.

## DISCOUNTING TICKETS

Having an audience means having to give discounts, too. Money can still be made for the Friends group through discounted tickets to Friends members. You can have two prices, one for members and one for nonmembers. If, for example, the membership fee is $10 annually, charge $35 for *two* tickets to the dinner. For nonmembers, charge $25 a plate, or some other amount that is higher than the member price.

Entire tables should be discounted for nonmembers also, but only enough so that the total cost is less than buying eight separate $25 tickets. Only groups who fill up a table of eight or multiples of eight should be discounted. Some Friends groups might be tempted to place ten to a table, but unless the tables are longer than standard, this usually results in crowding. A schedule of ticket costs should be placed in the ticket book for easy reference.

Don't forget to advertise the meal itself. One week before the event, an ad might be placed in the local paper advertising the event's menu. This can bring in several more guests if they see what they will get for their ticket price.

Arranging the tables also presents a problem. If the Friends group is attached to an academic library, *don't* think a call to the grounds crew will take care of the problem! All important matters, like fire escapes and handicapped access, need to be checked off a list. In addition to this, all of the tables must be positioned so that everyone can see and hear the speaker while still providing maximum seating (and revenue) for the Friends program.

One quick way to solve table arranging is to scout out the floor plan ahead of time. If possible, get a scale drawing of the floor plan and put cardboard tables on the drawing (to scale). This will provide a picture of where the tables should go and how many the room will accommodate without a complete set-up.

## BUFFET OR SIT-DOWN DINNER?

Are guests to be served, or will they go through a buffet line? For most groups, the simplest thing to do is to have guests go through a buffet line. It really doesn't matter, though the served meal always provides for a much better atmosphere.

| Name | Address | Phone Number | No. of tickets | Paid y/n | Date Mailed | Amt. Rec'd. | Comments |
|------|---------|--------------|----------------|----------|-------------|-------------|----------|
| Bass | 21 Fish Rd. | 967-1234 | 8 | y | 2/6/92 | $200 | reserve |
| Smith | 10 Jones | 764-1234 | 10 | y | 2/9/92 | $250 | reserve |
|  |  |  |  |  |  |  |  |
|  |  |  |  |  |  |  |  |
|  |  |  |  |  |  |  |  |
|  |  |  |  |  |  |  |  |

Figure 8-1. Sample Ticket Book Entries

In an academic setting, students may be used to serve the meal. In other settings, catering help, if the membership does not have enough volunteers, will be necessary. Depending on your budget, the latter may prove too costly, so a buffet-style dinner may be the only manageable option.

## TRAINING WAITERS AND WAITRESSES

If students or volunteers are used to serve, they need to be trained. Train them in everything from telling them how to serve to how to dress. This may seem presumptuous to some, but many students (and some volunteers) will appreciate the instruction.

The general rule of thumb on servers is ten servers for every 125 guests. This tends to overestimate the number needed, so once the servers are together, have a run-through to see if they step all over one another. Reduce the number if necessary.

## MISCELLANEOUS AUDIENCE ARRANGEMENTS

Other matters relating to the audience and the tables include folding chairs for all the guests, ticket-takers at the door, and change at the door for those who pay when they pick up their tickets. It's a good idea to have one table set up for those who must pay for their tickets and another for those who have already paid.

With the tables set and the arrangements on the tables, is everything ready? Not quite. Place at each setting a program for the evening. This helps the audience know what is coming and when. If the speech has a title, note it on the program. This program also provides a place to identify the head table and offer any more advertising or acknowledgment of those who have helped. Although programs add to the mess to be cleaned up when the dust settles and everyone leaves, they lessen audience befuddlement.

Another nice touch is music between all the different parts of the evening. Don't expect any talented musician to play for free. Of course, classical (or other types of) taped music may be used, but this requires a rather sophisticated amplification system if it is to be heard over the din of happy eaters.

# SPECIAL EVENTS

If a reception or tea is held in honor for the speaker, and guests are specially invited, preparations must be for made for that, too. This is by no means necessary, but it does make the annual event more special. A tea or a reception to introduce the speaker to faculty members, trustees, or special guests is a nice touch. Such an event may be held in the afternoon, perhaps two hours in advance of the dinner event. Or, it may be held as a reception after the event. When holding even a brief reception after the dinner, be sure not to keep your speaker (and your audience) too late.

Receptions for very special speakers can also give an added boost to your fundraising efforts. For example, sponsorships could be offered for $100 or $150. For these sponsorships, Friends groups might receive an invitation to a special reception following the dinner.

Teas or receptions mean getting napkins, service for the tea, servers, nuts, and "finger foods." This requires enlisting the dining hall or the caterer yet again. Because a tea is a small event, it is not beyond the reach of any library with five or more staff members. Keep the food simple and the service elegant, but not expensive. Don't use paper cups or any other inexpensive looking service. Usually, a library attached to a college or university will be able to find a tea service on campus. Other types of libraries will surely be able to find a service they can borrow.

# ORGANIZING THE TROOPS

How many people are needed to pull off an annual event, with all the bells and whistles? Let's add it up:

Servers: 25+ (depending on the number of guests anticipated)
Ticket takers: 3
Reception: 5
Total: 33

Since most of these people will come from either the library staff, the dining hall staff, the volunteer pool, or the catering company, the minimum number you have to supply is about 15.

# THINGS TO DO

Go through the checklist below, preparing each item as needed for a mock (or real) dinner. The items marked with asterisks are optional.

**ARRANGEMENTS CHECKLIST:**

1. Transportation to and from the airport and the hotel arranged.
2. Menu set.
3. Ticket book prepared.
4. Tickets printed.
5. Letters to special guests sent.
6. Head table seating done; cards made.
7. Arrangements for the tables made.
8. Arrangements for the head table made.
9. Librarian's closing remarks prepared (including auctioning of table arrangements).
10. Program for the tables done.*
11. Servers arranged.
12. Servers trained.
13. Ticket-takers lined up.
14. Press conference notices written and mailed.*
15. Room for the press conference secured.*
16. Reception food and miscellaneous items arranged.*
17. Invitations to the reception sent.*
18. Servers for the reception lined up.*
19. Speaker's return to hotel arranged.
20. Library prepared for the event.

# CLOSURE

## SIGNING OFF

Bringing an annual library event to an end is a serious business. The Friends leader's closing speech has to be, as we saw in the last chapter, short and sweet. It has also got to pack a punch. Although the speech will probably last no more than 15 minutes, it should pull everything together.

A few years ago, Ed Holley[1] pointed out that the academic librarian needs to know, or at least be cognizant of, three things in order to do a good job: professional skills, history, and politics. Any one of these might be a good place to end, but as with the invitation, so here with the closing, history of place provides a good point upon which to hang one's closing remarks at a Friends dinner.

What is the history of the library the Friends group is supporting? How was it founded? How did it come about? What is the historical context of the facility? Knowing the library's history and then expanding upon it as a close to a library event strikes a chord in almost everyone's heart. It may well be that the ancients were right after all. History *has* meaning because life has meaning.

Of course this isn't the *only* topic one can choose, but a closing talk should somehow connect the dinner to the library's purpose and needs. The talk may not be about the library at all. It can be a personal testimony of how important libraries have been to a Friends member, or someone from the community. The possibilities are limited only by your imagination. Don't make the mistake of thinking that closing remarks are unnecessary because it is obvious to everyone why they are there. These closing remarks should move listeners to act. They should make a point, and make it powerfully.

### THE FOLLOW-UP NEWSLETTER

A newsletter should be sent within *weeks* of the dinner's end. Your report on the dinner should include photos and a summary of what went on. This is the place to be more specific about library needs, or to elaborate on them if necessary. Newsletter articles, in addition to expanding on needs, should be explicit about how an individual can make a donation to any given project.

### MEMENTOS

Another way of maintaining interest in the group is to have small gifts to give away at the dinner, or even throughout the year. Pens, calendars, and other similar items are a great way to keep the audience remembering the Friends group and the library throughout the year.

## Mugs

A good way to create atmosphere and maintain interest in the library program is by offering commemorative mugs. Choose a nice-looking, durable mug, even if it means spending a little more money for it. Don't try to make a huge profit off of these mugs. One or two dollars above cost is plenty. One side of the mug might have the library's seal or motto. The other side might read "Friends of the Library," with the library's name (or the college or university's name, if an academic library) in colorful letters arching above the name of the speaker and the date that speaker appeared.

By including the speaker's name and the date, the Friends group provides an instant "collector's set" offering. If patrons buy one, they'll want to continue the set year after year.

## Sweatshirts

You could substitute sweatshirts for the mugs (or offer both if affordable). Fashion is always unpredictable, but sweatshirts have a timeless appeal. The front of the sweatshirt could have the library's name and logo or symbol, and the back could list the dates and speakers or events hosted by the Friends group. The question of whether to have them printed each year or every three or four years will be one the executive committee can decide on in collaboration with the program committee.

The idea behind mugs, pens, sweatshirts, and the like is to tantalize your audience. These items not only tantalize, but they also help to remind people about the library. If the Friends group puts on one major event each year, the need for reminders is imperative.

## BIMONTHLY PROGRAMS

Nothing stimulates the memory of a Friends group more than having smaller monthly or bimonthly programs, if the energy, money, and interest are there to sustain them. As discussed in the early chapters, putting on a Friends program, whether for 50 or 500 people, requires very nearly the same amount of preparation. If, however, the program committee members are game, these programs will offer ample material for each month's newsletter.

## KEEPING THE DREAM ALIVE

Once the annual program is over, the dust has settled, and it's Monday morning, the Friends committee members are basking in the glow of the wide and favorable publicity the program has received and go into hibernation until the next event, right? Wrong! The next step should be taken *that day*. The program cannot be shut down for two months or even two weeks. Granted, it is certainly taken off the front burner, but do not put it in moth balls.

## DISCOUNTING LEFTOVERS

You should try to sell whatever is left over from the dinner (mugs, flower arrangements, etc.) at the earliest possible date, at a discount if necessary. If the mailing list is too large for a letter to each member, you could take out a small ad in the local newspaper advertising what is left. If the group is attached to an academic library, send letters to faculty and staff. If a public library, try those city government publications that were used for publicity. This letter should give a time and place for viewing the "leftovers."

## COST ANALYSIS

Expenses should be added up and subtracted from income as soon as possible following the dinner to get one measure of success. Income should, of course, include *all* the money from the dinner: tickets, mugs, sweatshirts, arrangements—in short, everything sold in connection with the dinner. *All* of the expenses should then be subtracted from the income. While only one measure, it is probably the one administrators and trustees will be eager to know. Of course, the real measure of success as far as Friends committee members are concerned is progress toward the group's stated purposes. But this "bottom line" figure will carry significant weight with those to whom the group must report.

## MEETINGS WITH STAFF AND BOARD MEMBERS

Soon after the dinner (within ten days) the Friends leader should meet with the library staff and the executive board to get their impressions. Find out first if they thought the event was worthwhile. If the answer is yes, ask them what they thought worked well, what did not, and what changes they would like to see. Do not ask for suggestions, though, unless you intend to consider them seriously. Try to implement good suggestions at your next annual event, and acknowledge those who made them.

If the library staff's response to the dinner event is negative, the Friends leader and executive board will need to assess the strength of this resentment. If objections can be worked out, so much the better. If not, the program may have to be postponed until a more enthusiastic library staff comes on board, or run itself independently of the library. Independent Friends groups do exist, but the relationship between the library and the organization can be strained. Unfortunately, independent Friends groups sometimes end up in a power struggle between the leaders and the librarians. When this occurs, not only are there no winners, the library is the biggest loser of all.

## LETTERS TO SPEAKERS

Write a follow-up letter thanking the speaker and asking him or her to suggest changes that would help the program. Sure, the speaker has been paid, but courtesy is no crime. If possible, send the speaker birthday and Christmas cards each year. This added touch, while small and seemingly insignificant, will yield benefits over the years.

## CLEARING UP PROBLEMS

It is not a very enviable task, but one important aspect of "day after" cleanup is dealing with whatever problems occurred during the event. Someone may have been piqued by his table location, a family member may have been left out of ticket arrangements, a Friends volunteer may have tried to push his or her benefit too far. Such problems cannot be ignored. Some may require sending a note of apology or even a token gift along with a letter. Failure to handle these problems can result in "festering lilies."

## MAKING REPORTS

Other "day after" duties include making a report to the powers that be about the event. In an academic setting, this means the library director, the dean, the vice president or the president. In public libraries it means the library trustees, the librarian, and, possibly, important city officials.

But be sure to report the infinite value of publicity. People coming together under one roof to celebrate reading and libraries cannot be overrated. If the "take" turns out to be small, remind those to whom the report is sent that "250 people gathered last week to celebrate the library and its services."

The Friends groups should have two accounts, one that records all income and another that records all expenditures. Having both an income *and* an expenditure account helps to determine more precisely what was spent and what was taken in. Once the Friends group begins making money on its annual event, it is a good idea to leave $1,000 or $2,000 in the account for the next annual extravaganza.

## FOLLOW UP LETTERS TO THE MEDIA

If no more programs are planned for the year, and a newsletter is too costly, then you should write a letter to the editor of the local newspaper one week after the event thanking everyone for all their help. Silence kills, in this case, so keep Friends activities before the public as often as possible.

## THE TIME VERSUS EFFORT QUESTION

The last matter to discuss with committee members and especially the library staff is time. Friends groups do consume lots of time. Often volunteers will be missing and the Friends leader will have to fill in. In a small town, the librarian will have to take on more and more of the responsibilities of the Friends group. Is it worth it? Of course it is, a thousand times over. But not everyone will be in agreement. The Friends leader and committee members need to assess how much time is too much. Unless the first dinner is an absolute fiasco from start to finish, however, this decision should not be made until after two or three annual events have taken place.

## FINAL BUDGETS

The Friends leader will need to present a final budget to whatever the appropriate groups may be. These could include, but are not limited to, presidents, chairs of boards of trustees, library directors, and, of course, the broader Friends memberships. The budget worksheet discussed in chapter 6 can be adapted for the final report. When viewing such reports, administrators will want to see "bottom line" figures. It is impractical to expect profits *every* year. Even the most profitable Fortune 500 companies have "off" years. So, when making this final report, be sure to include a budget line for "in-kind" income. In-kind income may include publicity for the library or good will spread throughout the community. Failure to report such "income" will tempt administrators to look with jaundiced eyes at the Friends activities during those inevitable "off" years.

## SCRAPBOOK

Press releases, news stories, menus, programs, and newsletters can produce quite a bit of history. Ask a member to keep a scrapbook on all Friends-related activities and press clippings. A scrapbook can be put to many uses, not the least of which is showing off your huge success to trustees and administrators.

# THINGS TO DO

1.  Research the library's history for facts that might be put to use in a closing speech.

2.  Read Holley's article "Defining the Academic Librarian" (see bibliography). Also, look through the publication *Library Literature* under the heading, "Librarians and Librarianship" for other helpful articles.

3.  Assess any annual events you have already had, whether or not they were connected with the library. Were they successful? Why or why not?

4.  Talk over the amount of time it takes to plan and execute an annual event with your staff and committee members. Is this too much time in return for the effort?

5.  Between big annual events, try having book sales, bake sales and other similar activities to supplement the Friends income account.

# ENDNOTE

1. Ed Holley, "Defining the Academic Librarian," *College and Research Libraries* 46: 462-468.

# 10 TWENTY QUESTIONS

You've made it through all the planning stages, set up committees, gotten your Friends group moving, planned your first annual event, and done all the follow-up—at least in your mind. Now it's time to make sure you're really ready to organize a Friends group and plan events. If you know the answers to the following 20 questions, you'll be well on your way.

## 1. Should the library director support the Friends organization?

Yes! If the current director does not support the idea of a Friends group, it may be best to wait for a new director. If the director does support the group, you should let him or her know what it will involve. The work is substantial, the time constraints great. But with planning, a lot of energy, and the desire to see the library surpass its budget goals, Friends groups are a great way of achieving something permanent for the library. It's important that the library director realize this.

## 2. What preparations need to be made in order to initiate a Friends group?

After preparing yourself first, you should be sure that the library staff is prepared. Are they ready to spend extra hours working on a venture that, in the beginning, produces very little in the way of results for bottom line-minded individuals? One way to check on staff readiness is to look at their job performance and attitudes now.

The next step is to assess the leadership element in the community. Are there one or two individuals who could act as a Friends leader? After that, the steering committee must be formed, the kickoff event organized, and so on, down to the first annual event.

## 3. What's the best approach for organizing a group?

One best approach doesn't exist. Because people like to feel that they have some say in determining the future (insofar as it will involve them), a participative approach usually works quite well. In participative decision making, the cadre of people who will work to put things together *share* in the decision-making process.

This participative management approach will also be carried over later into the larger, fully functioning group, where decisions will not be made regardless of group wishes, or without group consent, but will be made with as much input as the group wishes to have. Participation also means that those who do not wish to participate will not be made to. A leader must be found with enough energy and vision to oversee the majority of operations so that all library personnel are in the background, working no less hard, but out of the limelight.

### 4. What type of Friends group should be initiated?

In order to find out what kind of group will work best, the Friends organizer needs to do a market survey in miniature. Find out something about the community.

The market survey looks at a number of things, such as radio programming (i.e., the kind of music played and the most successful stations), what sells well in the area (pick-up trucks, Cadillacs, or both), and what is produced *locally* on television. It is also a good idea to look at the number of civic clubs and churches. These things mean nothing individually, but together they make a collective statement about the community.

### 5. How does one go about forming the nucleus of the group?

The first thing to do is to get several dozen names using a variety of sources: a development office, friends, trustees, or even from circulation records. Once you have a list of these people, you should research their participation in similar Friends groups. Once the executive board has been selected, plan some kind of kickoff event, such as a tea. You should schedule the event at a time that is festive. Perhaps the library is commemorating its anniversary, or it's National Library Week. Choose a time that will get people in the mood for getting out, but not a season when all sorts of events vie for their time.

At this event, be prepared to tell your guests the plans for the Friends group. Obviously, this means there must be some. A general plan will have come out of the work of the steering committee and the executive board. You might set up volunteer sign-up sheets at the tea so that people are able to sign up for work immediately. But do not leave everything to chance. Have on hand the names of Friends leaders who are willing to help and present their names as potential Friends leaders.

Another way to gain members is to publish a Friends newsletter. It may seem odd to publish a newsletter before there is a group, but if no other vehicle is available (such as a regular library newsletter, a college or university bulletin, or a public library news sheet), then a newsletter is a must unless someone is willing to call everyone on the phone. The "lead" story should be the announcement that a group is forming and that an informational tea will be held. If a newsletter is not possible, you might consider taking out an ad in the community newspaper.

## 6. When is the group ready to "go public"?

Although it is impossible to say how many months one should wait before getting a group started, or resuming a group that has been dormant for a number of years, it's generally a good idea to wait until the following requirements are met. First, the library director must be fully supportive of the idea. Second, a Friends leader who is familiar with the community must be found who will nurse the organization to full maturity. If the library director is new to the community and the library, one year is about the minimum amount of time to wait before launching a Friends group, unless the skeletal organization of one is already present.

## 7. How are all of the Friends committees put to work for the annual event?

This can't be done very well without first getting a cadre of people together and talking. The market survey should provide information regarding the kind of annual event to have. Once that has been determined, at least six months should be set aside to pull it together. Do not make any announcement about the annual event until it is certain. Delegation is the key word. The Friends leader must delegate the activities (publicity, arrangements, transportation, tables, etc.) to committees but oversee all of it.

## 8. How is interest sustained when the annual event is eight months away?

A newsletter can help with this problem. If publishing a newsletter is not possible, then perhaps you could undertake some smaller fundraising activities and announce them in the local newspaper. These could be things like book sales, readathons, or any other activity that will draw attention to the library and its work.

### 9. How is the community alerted to the Friends group?

One way to do this is to make sure power brokers have been identified and contacted. Another way is to make the Friends group a vehicle for all outside library activity. Make certain, whenever it is reasonable to do so, that Friends' activities are linked to the library's work. If someone asks how they can help the library, tell them, "Join our Friends group." Whenever either the Friends leader or the librarian is called on to speak about *anything*, be sure a comment or two about the library's Friends group is inserted at some point. This may seem like evangelical zeal about library work, but new enterprises must be talked about often. If Friends leaders don't do it, who will?

### 10. What about "foot draggers" who may end up on the executive board?

The answer is simple: confront them. Forget trying to leave messages through others, beating around the bush, or hinting in a joco-serious manner. Be kind, but direct. Don't allow anyone to "drop the ball." Point out their misstep in a courteous, but direct, manner.

### 11. How does a Friends group land "big name" speakers?

In this area, it helps if there is a bit of the ham in the Friends leader. Be bold, be daring. Ask anybody who the committee thinks would make for a dazzling program.

Search through biographical indexes for speakers suitable to the program and community and write to them. Limit the letter to one page, and try to come up with an opening that is positive and interesting. Talk about money later, not in the initial letter. The main idea is to get the speaker to come, or at least to get him or her in the right frame of mind to consider coming.

### 12. Wouldn't using a speaker's bureau be a lot easier?

Yes and no. Yes, because they will make the first contact with the speaker for you and do a lot of the legwork. No, because they will increase overall costs and will make for frustrating three-way communications. The fewer people there are between the Friends leader and the speaker, the better.

## 13. How important is publicity?

It's hard to say that any one thing in a Friends production is more important than another, but if one thing should be, it is publicity. Rely on publicity for everything: to get people interested in the group; to gain new members; to advertise the annual event; and to sustain interest in it during the year. If publicity is not taken seriously, the rest of your work may be much more difficult.

It is best to think in terms of publicizing in *every* way possible, rather than thinking of how many places can be omitted. This means publicizing in the traditional ways—radio, television, newspapers—and the not so traditional ways—friends newsletters, posters, civic groups, and churches.

## 14. What sort of arrangements need to be made for the dinner?

In fine Aristotelian manner, think in terms of categories: speaker, dining hall, tables, accommodations, transportation (by air, by land), after-dinner arrangements, and follow-up. If you break activities down in this manner, everything will remain in fairly decent order.

If necessary, glance back to the chapter on arrangements for details, but here's a basic list of the things you need to consider: the sound system, the space needed for the guests to sit, the number of guests, the quality and quantity of food, waiters and waitresses (optional), music (optional), closing comments, table arrangements, flight schedules, transportation to and from the dinner site to the hotel, hotel accommodations, receptions, teas, and the big send-off.

## 15. Should there be a head table, and who should sit there?

Yes, and those who should sit at the head table, in addition to the Friends leader, are those who have played an instrumental part in bringing the dinner about, and those who make the dinner possible. For an academic library, this means a seat for the president of the institution (and possibly the vice president), the president and vice president of the Friends group, the librarian or library director, and the speaker. For special and public libraries, replace the president and vice president with board of trustees members, such as the chair of the board and the secretary, and perhaps one or two important city officials.

More than ten at a head table complicates matters and confuses audiences. Try to keep the number to ten or fewer.

### 16. What about the press and free tickets?

The press will either be a big ally or a big headache. A good policy is to offer two free tickets: one for the reporter and one for a cameraman or photographer. If the press asks for more "comps," don't be afraid to ask why they need more. Are they going to do a feature story? When will it run? How many pictures will there be? Radio stations should need only one ticket.

Above all, get to know reporters! Have the library director invite them out to the library, be a source of information to them, and give them a user's card if they do not already have one. Potential press frustrations can be defused by doing these things early on.

### 17. Are political entities important to a humble Friends group?

Whether the Friends group is humble or haughty, political entities are important. Politics isn't everything, but everything is politics, or so it would seem. These political considerations *must* be recognized, or the group will suffer unnecessarily. The best way to go about uncovering the political structure in a community is to interview key groups using one or more of the methods outlined in chapter 3 (positional, reputational, or decision-making). Once groups or individuals have been identified, the Friends organizer can learn how to "break into" the political power base, using whatever he or she needs for the benefit of the library and the Friends group.

### 18. Do small groups need to bother with all this?

Certainly it is possible to have a group of people gather around the online catalog or a computer terminal and trade book stories. Or, perhaps holding forth on an arcane academic matter is more to one's fancy. One approach is not inherently better than another, but which one will produce funds? If the Friends group wants to achieve more than camaraderie, it'll need a significant effort behind it to secure it.

### 19. When is it time to give up?

Not every group is going to be successful. Mark Twain once advised an aspiring writer to work at writing for three years. If it wasn't paying him by the end of that time, Twain said that he should try something else. Two to three years should be plenty of time to get a Friends group up and running.

### 20. Why begin a Friends group at all?

Friends groups help to mobilize the library in the community. Since everything *is* politics, libraries need to begin *today* to make sure political machinations will not remove them from the public square. Institutions that take themselves for granted, and their place in culture as secure, often find they have been overlooked or bypassed later.

Many librarians tend to think this way. They reason that books and reading are so important that no one in their right mind would think of putting them out of business. No one does put them out of business *deliberately*. What happens instead is that libraries get saddled as cost-ineffective operations, so they get cut. But why are they saddled with that charge? *Because no one is out there telling people that the library is an essential factor in the community's cultural and economic well-being.*

Libraries are the nation's guardians against ignorance and illiteracy. They shine the light of truth in a world full of darkness. But libraries need a helping hand. Friends groups may offer that succor. A Friends group—whether its primary raison d'etre is good fun, highbrow ruminations and serious discussions, or just raising money for the library—serves the community by helping it to see what it has in its libraries. Friends groups exist to ensure that the light of libraries is never extinguished.

# BIBLIOGRAPHY

Agger, R., D. Goldrich and B. Swanson. *The Rulers and the Ruled.* New York: John Wiley and Sons, Inc., 1964.

Aiken, M., and P. Mott. *The Structure of Community Power.* New York: Random House, 1970.

*The ALA Yearbook of Library and Information Services.* Chicago: American Library Association. (See "Friends of Libraries" entry in each edition.)

Bachrach, S.B., and E.J. Lauler. *Power and Politics in Organizations.* San Francisco: Jossey Bass, 1980.

Barnett, A., and P. Brownell. "Misapplications Reviews: The Mystery of the Two-faced Regression." *Interfaces* 19 (March-April 1989): 56-60.

Bartunek, J., and C. Kepys. "Participation in School Decision Making." *Urban Education* 14 (1979): 52-75.

Belsky, K. "Callaway Library Gets a Little Help from Its Friends." *Show-Me Libraries* 37 (August 1986): 508.

Bennis, W. *The Planning of Change.* New York: Holt, Rinehart and Winston, 1976.

Biscos, S. "Employee Participation without Pain." *HR Magazine* (April 1990): 89-90.

Bishop, R. "What Newspapers Say about Public Relations." *Public Relations Review* 14 (Summer 1988): 50-52.

Brawner, L., and E. Clark. "Anatomy of a Library's Experience with Four Book Sales." *Public Library Quarterly* 6 (Fall 1985): 9-24.

Campbell, R., and W. Wayson. "Decision-Making in the Elementary Principalship." *National Elementary Principal* 41 (1962): 17-22.

Cotton, J. (and others). "Employee Participation: Diverse Forms and Different Outcomes." *The Academy of Management Review* (January 1988): 8-22.

Cox, A. "Everybody Wins with Teamwork." *Across the Board* 26 (May 1989): 9-10.

Daft, R. L. *Organizational Theory and Design.* St. Paul, Minn.: West Publishing, 1983.

Dahl, R. *Modern Political Analysis.* New York: Prentice Hall, 1984.

————. *Who Governs: Democracy and Power in an American City*. New Haven, Conn.: Yale University Press, 1961.

Day, D. "Make the Most of Meetings." *Personnel Journal* (March 1990): 34.

Dolnick, S. *Friends of Libraries Sourcebook*. Chicago: American Library Association, 1980.

————. "Friends of Libraries." *Library Association Record* 89 (March 1987): 139.

D'Souza, D. *Illiberal Education*. New York: Free Press, 1991.

Edwards, M. "A Joint Effort Leads to Accurate Appraisals." *Personnel Journal* 69 (June 1990): 122.

Eldredge, J. "More Valuable Than Money: Outstanding Friends Groups Hailed." *College and Research Libraries News* 52, No. 10: 635-639.

Friends of Libraries USA. *Friends of Libraries National Notebook*. Chicago: American Library Association, 1989.

Frohman, M. "Participative Management: What It Takes to Make It Work." *Industry Week* 236 (May 2, 1988): 37-38.

Furlow, K., and A. McArthur. "Friends of the Library." *College and Research Libraries* 36 (July 1975): 272-282.

Haeuser, M. "What Friends Are For: Gaining Financial Independence." *Wilson Library Bulletin* 60 (May 1986): 25-27.

Herman, S. "Participative Management Is a Double-Edged Sword." *Training* (January 1989): 52-53.

Hoerr, J. "The Payoff from Teamwork." *Business Week* (July 10, 1989): 56-62.

Holley, E. "Defining the Academic Librarian." *College and Research Libraries* 46 (1985): 462-468.

"How to Get Press Attention." *Venture* 9 (December 1987): 20.

Hunter, F. *Community Power Structure*. Chapel Hill: University of North Carolina Press, 1953.

Janis, I.L. *Groupthink: Psychological Studies of Policy Decisions and Fiascoes*. Boston: Houghton Mifflin, 1982.

————. *Victims of Groupthink*. Boston: Houghton Mifflin, 1972.

Katz, W. *The How-to-Do-It Manual for Small Libraries*. New York: Neal-Schuman, 1988.

Kimbrough, R. *Political Power and Educational Decision-Making*. Chicago: Rand McNally and Company, 1970.

Kochoff, S. "Alternative Funding Sources: Friends as Fund Raisers." *Bottom Line* 3, No. 1 (1989): 35-36.

Krummel, D. W. (ed.). *Organizing the Library's Support: Donors, Volunteers, Friends*. Urbana-Champaign: University of Illinois Press, 1980.

Lasswell, H. *The Signature of Power: Buildings, Communication, and Policy*. New Brunswick, N.J.: Transactions Books, 1979.

Levin, D. "Publicizing the Impossible." *Public Relations Journal* 45 (February 1989): 30-31.

Lewin, K. "Frontiers in Group Dynamics I. Concepts, Methods, and Reality in Social Science: Social Equilibrium and Social Change." *Human Relations* 1 (1947): 1-39.

Linzer, L. "How to Use Research to Get Publicity." *Public Relations Journal* 44 (December 1988): 29-31.

Lipsett, S. "The Academic Mind at the Top: The Political Behavior and Values of Faculty Elites." *Public Opinion Quarterly* 46 (1982): 143-168.

Lowin, A. "Participative Decision Making: A Model, Literature Critique, and Prescriptions for Research." *Organizational Behavior and Human Performance* 3 (1968): 68-106.

Margulies, N., and S. Black. "Perspectives on the Implementation of Participative Approaches." *Human Resource Management* (Fall 1987): 385-412.

Muczyk, J., and B. Reinmann. "Has Participative Management Been Oversold?" *Personnel* (May 1987): 52-56.

Mugny, G. *The Power of Minorities*. New York: Academic Press, 1982.

Musman, V.K. "Managerial Style in a Small Public Library." *California Librarian* (July 1978): 7-20.

Ney, N., and E. Brownlee. "Alice B. Toklas and the Liberries: Building a Successful Friends Group." *Library Journal* 113 (February 1, 1988): 41-43.

Pascarella, P. "There's No Escaping It: Worker Participation Is Becoming Standard Practice." *Industry Week* 238 (January 16, 1989): 7.

Paulette, E. "That's What Friends Are For! Activities of FOL Groups in the Northwest Chapter." *Ohio Library Association Bulletin* 57 (October 1987): 17-19.

Phillips, J. "Implementing Participative Management." *Supervision* 49 (August 1987): 3-5.

Presthus, R. *Men at the Top: A Study in Community Power*. New York: Oxford University Press, 1964.

Rothman, S. "Academics on the Left." *Society* 23, No. 3 (1986): 4-8.

Shapiro, I., and G. Reeher. *Power, Inequity, and Democratic Politics: Essays in Honor of Robert A. Dahl*. Boulder and London: Westview Press, 1988.

SPEC Kit #94. *Fund Raising in ARL Libraries*. Washington: Association of Research Libraries, 1983.

Spector, B. "From Bogged Down to Fired Up: Inspiring Organizational Change." *Sloan Management Review* 30 (Summer 1989): 29-34.

Stead, J. "Tap Your People's Power: U.S. Business Needs Greater Employee Involvement." *Industry Week* 239 (April 2, 1990): 32.

"Ten Tips for Preparing Guest Speakers: Good Advice from the Connecticut Friends," No. 61 (1986): 27.

Thompson, R. (comp.). *Friends of College Libraries*. CLIP Note #9. Washington: Association of Research Libraries, 1987.

Tjosbold, D. "Participation: A Close Look at Its Dynamics." *Journal of Management* (Winter 1987): 739-750.

Toffler, A. *Powershift: Knowledge, Wealth, and Violence at the Edge of the 21st Century*. New York: Bantam Books, 1990.

Torbert, R. "Friends of Libraries." In *The ALA Yearbook of Library and Information Services*, v. 13, (1988): 142-144.

Verespej, M. "Success in the '90s: The Key Is People." *Industry Week* 239 (May 7, 1990): 35-36.

"Want Your Story Told? Then Make Life Easy for Reporters." *Marketing News* 21 (October 9, 1987): 7.

Welsh, W. *Leaders and Elites.* New York: Holt, Rinehart and Winston, 1979.

Williams, G. "The Public Library as Publishers: Some Scissors, Rubber Cement, and Time." *Wilson Library Bulletin* 61 (June 1987): 34-35.

Wood, C.J. "Participative Decision Making: Why Doesn't It Seem to Work?" *Educational Forum*, 49 (1984): 55-64.

Zander, A. *Making Groups Effective.* San Francisco: Jossey Bass, 1982.

# INDEX

Mark Y. Herring is Dean of Library Services and Director of the Mabee Learning Center at Oklahoma Baptist University, Shawnee, Oklahoma.

Book design: Gloria Brown
Cover design: Apicella Design
Typography: C. Roberts